ANCIENT CIVILIZATIONS

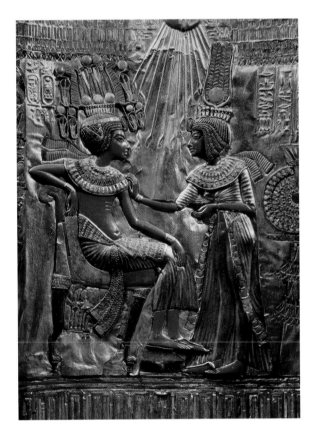

VOLUME 10

TOOLS AND TECHNOLOGY—WRITING

GROLIER
EDUCATIONAL

Published by Grolier Educational
Sherman Turnpike
Danbury, Connecticut 06816

© 2000 Brown Partworks Ltd

Set ISBN: 0-7172-9471-4
Volume ISBN: 0-7172-9481-1

Library of Congress Cataloging-in-Publication Data
Ancient civilizations.
    p. cm. — Includes bibliographical references and indexes.
    Summary: A multi-volume encyclopedia with alphabetically
arranged topics relating to ancient civilizations and the
discovery of famous archaeological sites.
    ISBN 0-7172-9471-4 (set: alk. paper). — ISBN 0-7172-9472-2
(v. 1: alk. paper). — ISBN 0-7172-9473-0 (v. 2: alk. paper). —
ISBN 0-7172-9474-9 (v. 3: alk. paper).
    1. Civilization. Ancient Encyclopedias, Juvenile. 2. Prehistoric
peoples Encyclopedias, Juvenile. 3. Antiquities Encyclopedias,
Juvenile. 4. Excavations (Archaeology) Encyclopedias, Juvenile.
[1. Civilization, Ancient Encyclopedias. 2. Prehistoric peoples
Encyclopedias. 3. Antiquities Encyclopedias. 4. Excavations
(Archaeology) Encyclopedias. 5. Archaeology Encyclopedias.]
    I. Grolier Educational (Firm)
CB311.A5197   2000   99-28387
930—dc21   CIP

For information address the publisher:
Grolier Educational, Sherman Turnpike,
Danbury, Connecticut 06816

FOR BROWN PARTWORKS LTD

Project editor: Shona Grimbly
Design: Wilson Design Associates
Picture research: Veneta Bullen
Text editors: Chris King
                       Sally MacEachern
Managing editor: Lindsey Lowe
Consultant: Paul Bahn

Printed in Singapore

Maps

The maps in this book show you the locations of cities and sites of the
distant past. Ancient cities and sites are shown by red dots, while
modern-day cities and sites are shown by black dots.

Ancient place names and names of countries are shown in bold type,
while modern place and country names are shown in ordinary type.

About this book

This is one of a set of 10 books telling the stories of the
peoples and civilizations of the distant past. Thousands
of years ago hunter-gathering peoples began to settle
down in villages and start to farm. They also began to
develop many remarkable skills. They learned to make
clay into bricks and pots, they learned to mine metals
and fashion them into ornaments, tools, and weapons,
and they learned how to weave cloth out of the fibers
of plants. In a surprisingly short time some of these
peoples were living in large cities and were trading
with other people great distances away.

The books in this set relate these achievements and
also describe some of the notable inventions that
helped human beings along the road to civilization,
such as the wheel, the compass—and sanitation. Some
of the entries in this book describe a particular
people or civilization in depth, while other entries take
a subject, such as "Numbers and Counting," and
examine it across a range of civilizations. Other entries
look at archaeological sites of special interest and tell
the story of their discovery. The entries are arranged
alphabetically and are illustrated with photographs,
drawings, and maps. Each entry ends with a list of
cross-references to other entries in the set. At the end
of the book there is an illustrated timeline to help you
relate the civilizations to each other in time. There is
also a useful "Further Reading" list and an index
covering the whole set.

CONTENTS

TOOLS AND TECHNOLOGY

Some animals use tools and even, to a very limited extent, make them. Chimpanzees, our closest living relatives, select twigs and break them to a suitable shape so they can use them to fish termites out of their mounds. Our earliest ancestors must also have used and slightly modified natural materials such as wood and bone to help them get food. This required thinking ahead to work out the job to be done and what the tool needed to be like.

Early hominids (our ancestors) lived on a variety of foods. They included dead animals, which they scavenged. Other scavengers had sharp teeth, claws, or beaks, but hominids didn't. So to cut through the tough hides of dead creatures to get at the meat, around 2.5 million years ago our ancestors began making sharp-edged stone tools. This required planning skills. The hominids who made stone tools needed to be able to think of using a sharp edge for cutting, imagine how to make a tool by striking pieces off the edge of a rock, and then do so, hitting the rock

▲ *A 19th-century artist's impression of cave dwellers in the early Stone Age. The men on the right are making simple tools out of stone. On the left a group of women use stone scrapers to clean a hide.*

exactly the correct way to make the pieces come off as wanted.

Stone tools were made by flaking pieces of stone off a small rock. At first, the toolmakers struck the pebble using what is known as a hammerstone. As time went on, however, they discovered that using a softer hammer made of wood or bone gave them greater control over the way they removed the flakes, allowing them to make the shape they wanted more exactly.

Still greater control could be achieved by using a scraping motion on the pebble to remove flakes rather than using the direct force of a blow. These techniques enabled people to create efficient tools using smaller and smaller pieces of stone. Large flakes gave way to smaller blades from which were made a range of different tools. Stone knives and axes made it easier for people to kill animals to get food. Sometimes axes were held in the hand; sometimes they were attached to

wooden handles. Awls were used for piercing leather, scrapers for cleaning hides, and chisels for working wood.

By 8000 B.C. people in many parts of the world were using microliths— tiny sharp pieces of stone that they could use as part of many different tools. For example, a row of microliths fastened into a piece of bone or wood formed a sickle, a sharp tool for cutting reeds, grasses, and cereal stalks. Microliths were also used to tip arrows made of wood and were made into drill bits for making holes in stone beads.

WORKING METALS

The discovery of how to extract metals from their ores was a major advance in the history of toolmaking. The first metal to be smelted, or removed from its ore by heating, was copper. This discovery was made around 6000 B.C. in western Asia and southeastern Europe. However, copper was too soft a material to be used to make effective

▼ *Iron tools were stronger than those made out of bronze. This collection of Celtic iron farming tools, from the first century B.C., includes a hoe, sickle, and ax heads. They would all originally have been attached to wooden handles.*

tools, and it was not until it was mixed with tin to make bronze that useful metal tools could be made. Bronze was first produced in the Middle East around 3500 B.C. and was used to make both farming implements and weapons.

Bronze had one major drawback. The tin needed to produce it was not widely available. Another ore, that of iron, was much more widespread, although it was more difficult to separate the metal from its ore. Once people learned how to do this around 1200 B.C., iron took over from bronze as the metal most commonly used for tools. It was superior to bronze in that it was stronger and could be shaped into a sharp cutting edge more easily.

What had prevented people from exploiting natural reserves of iron ore before was the fact that the metal only separated from its ore at very high temperatures, over 2800° F (1500° C). The production of iron only became possible when people discovered that they could reach far higher temperatures in their furnaces by using charcoal rather than wood as the fuel. Another important development was the introduction of bellows to increase temperatures still further.

FARMING TECHNOLOGY

As early civilizations began to evolve, simple pieces of machinery started to appear. Essentially, they served the same basic purpose as hand-held tools, allowing people to farm, hunt, and build houses more efficiently. The primary concern of all ancient peoples

▲ *This wall painting from an ancient Egyptian tomb shows carpenters using metal tools, including a saw and chisels, to work on a wooden sarcophagus. Both the saw and the chisel are examples of ancient tools that have altered little over the centuries.*

THE POTTER'S WHEEL

Pottery was one of the earliest crafts—people started making pots around 10,500 B.C. Originally, all pots were molded by hand without any technology, but gradually the potter's wheel evolved to make the process easier. At first, the wheel was balanced on a pivot in the ground and turned slowly by hand. However, this gradually developed into a more complicated device in which two separate wheels were connected—one at hand level on which the clay rested and one at foot level that was kicked to provide motion. This meant that the potter's hands were left free to mold the clay. We do not know exactly when and where the potter's wheel was invented, but it was certainly in use in Mesopotamia by 3500 B.C.

was producing enough food to eat, so it is not surprising that many of these technological developments occurred in the realm of agriculture.

One of the most important of these technical advances was the introduction of the ox-drawn plow. This device first appeared in Mesopotamia in around 4000 B.C. and quickly replaced the hand-held wooden hoes that had been used for centuries. It consisted of a V-shaped, wooden wedge joined to a wooden beam. Oxen were harnessed to the beam and used to haul the plow over the ground. The invention allowed far greater areas of land to be farmed than had been previously possible. The design was so efficient that it continued to be used until the 14th century A.D.

WATERING THE LAND

Another highly important development was the introduction of irrigation techniques. As early as 5000 B.C. irrigation channels were dug near the Nile River in Egypt and the Tigris and Euphrates rivers in Mesopotamia. They allowed the water from the annual floods to be diverted to fields to help crops grow. Dams were soon being built to store water during dry months. In order to raise water from the canals and reservoirs, a device known as a shadoof was invented. It consisted of a balanced beam with a bucket on one end and a counterweight on the other. It is still used in many parts of the world today.

The need to move water from one place to another became even greater when large cities started to develop. The Romans used an extensive system of aqueducts—open channels carrying water—to serve the needs of the growing urban population in their cities. These aqueducts usually brought water from a high natural source, such as a mountain spring, downhill to where it was needed, using the natural

force of gravity as propulsion. One famous aqueduct, the Aqua Marcia, was 57 miles (91km) long.

Occasionally, however, water would have to be forced uphill, and for this the Romans used siphons. Siphons were closed pipes that contained no pockets of air. Because of the pressure built up by the flow of water, they could be used to transmit it uphill for small distances. Both aqueducts and siphons were used by the earlier Greeks, but it was the Romans who developed them most fully.

LEVERS AND PULLEYS

In order to put up such huge structures, ancient builders often had to move large blocks of stone. This was

▼ *A modern reconstruction of the kind of forge used by Celtic metalworkers in around 200 B.C. Forges were used to fashion iron tools and weapons out of lumps of red-hot metal. In the center are the bellows that were used to fan the flames to increase the heat of the fire.*

WATER POWER

While human muscle was the most common source of power in the ancient world, it was not the only one. Water-powered machines are known to have been used by both the ancient Chinese and the Romans by the first century A.D. Chinese texts talk about a highly complex machine in which a waterwheel was used to power a set of bellows. According to the records, the device was invented by a man called Tu Shih in 31 A.D. However, it is likely that simpler versions of this machine were made much earlier.

Watermills are known to have been in widespread use in the Roman world. The most famous example is a flour mill at Barbégal in modern-day France. The mill was set on a sloping piece of ground, and water was carried to the top by an aqueduct. It then flowed downhill through two sets of eight waterwheels. The flow of the water turned the wheels, which were connected by a set of gears to machines for grinding corn. It has been estimated that 27 tons (30 tonnes) of corn were ground daily.

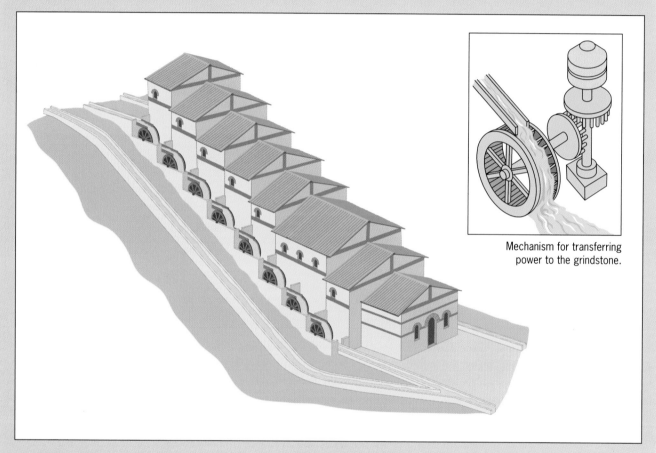

Mechanism for transferring power to the grindstone.

▲ *The Roman watermill at Barbégal, France, which was built around 300 A.D. On each side of the mill a stream of water flowed downhill through a series of eight waterwheels.*

made possible partly by the vast amount of slave labor available to many ancient civilizations, and partly by the development of simple devices and machines that increased the natural strength of human beings. Probably the oldest of these devices was the lever.

The simplest form of lever was a plank of wood resting on a point known as a fulcrum. By pressing down on one end of the lever, people were able to lift loads supported on the other end. People soon found that by moving the fulcrum closer to the load, they were

▲ *An artist's impression of a Roman crane, based on the writings of the engineer Vitruvius, who lived in the first century B.C. The crane is being used to lift heavy building blocks of stone and is powered by a treadmill worked by slaves.*

able to lift far greater weights with the same amount of effort. The ancient Egyptians used levers to help them build their pyramids.

Another simple device that helped people lift heavy objects was the pulley. A pulley consists of a piece of rope fitted over the rim of a wheel. Simple pulleys such as this allowed people to lift an object by pulling downward rather than upward. Systems of pulleys, with wheels of different sizes, allowed people to lift large weights with a comparatively small amount of effort. It is recorded that the Greek scientist Archimedes singlehandedly pulled a ship into the sea using a system of levers and pulleys.

Roman builders used the pulley as a central part of a machine that has survived to the present day—the crane. In Roman cranes the pulley was

attached to the end of a tall pole. Such cranes are described in the works of the Roman writer and engineer Vitruvius. The end of the rope farthest from the load was wound around a bar that was turned using a handle—a device known as a windlass. Like the pulley, the windlass reduced the amount of effort needed to move the load. Occasionally, cranes were connected to treadmills—large wheels powered by slaves walking inside them.

SEE ALSO:

◆ **IRRIGATION**
◆ **METALS**
◆ **SCIENCE**
◆ **TRANSPORTATION**
◆ **WARFARE AND WEAPONS**

TOWNS AND CITIES

Hunter-gatherers generally lived in quite small groups of about 20 to 30 people, since the plants and animals they depended on were usually spread thinly over a wide area. However, when people started to settle down in one place and farm, it was possible for them to live in larger communities. Sometimes these settlements grew to a great size, like Çatal Höyük, which flourished in Anatolia around 6000 B.C.

The first settlements were villages in which all the houses were much the same, and all the inhabitants lived by farming. As a village grew in size, it might become home to people with a variety of specialized occupations—a king, priests, merchants, and craftsmen, for instance, as well as farmers. It might also contain specialized buildings like

▲ *This artist's impression of the royal palace at Nimrud gives a good idea of how the magnificent palaces built by the Assyrian kings might have looked. Nimrud was the capital of the Assyrian Empire between about 880 and 707 B.C. To celebrate the completion of the palace, King Ashurnasirpal held a 10-day party for 70,000 guests.*

temples and a royal palace. At this point the village had become a town.

Towns first appeared in places where intensive farming made it possible for lots of people to get enough to eat from quite a small area, such as Mesopotamia and the Nile and Indus valleys. The surplus food that the farmers produced could feed other people who did not farm, such as craftsmen and merchants. Regular markets soon grew up where goods could be exchanged, and this gradually led to long-distance trade being developed.

THE RISE OF CITIES

Cities were generally larger and more complex than towns, and were often major political centers. In some regions and periods individual cities were the main settlement and the center of government for small, independent states, such as the city-states of ancient Greece and the Maya. In other places or periods larger states emerged, such as the Roman and Chinese empires. In them cities were the political and economic centers of regions under the authority of the ruler who was based in the capital city.

CHOICE OF LOCATION

Towns and cities developed in certain places and in particular ways for a number of reasons. Many grew up as a result of trade. These towns were located at key places on trade routes and became centers of crafts and industries. Other towns developed as political centers in areas of high population—they grew up at key places for controlling the surrounding area. Changed conditions brought changes in the location and importance of individual towns and cities. In China, for instance, under the Shang dynasty (1766–1100 B.C.) and Chou dynasty (1050–256 B.C.) state capitals were frequently moved when states won or lost wars with barbarians or rival states.

Religion was also influential in establishing towns, which might grow up around sacred sites. Such towns might provide accommodation for pilgrims, plus offerings and souvenirs for them to buy, as well as supplying the needs of the priests. Some remained largely religious centers, such as Delphi in Greece, where those who came to consult the oracle (the priestess of the god Apollo) left rich offerings. Others, such as the Mesoamerican city of Teotihuacán (which was built over a cave from which the first humans

▶ *Many of the first towns and cities were built out of mud bricks, a building material that was cheap and surprisingly durable. This form of building material is still used today, as this view of the city of Kano in Nigeria shows.*

were believed to have emerged), grew into major economic and political centers as well.

Most thriving settlements were located close to a good water supply and to land that could produce crops and support livestock. Frequently, they lay on good lines of communication, such as rivers, the sea, or routes through mountains; and, where appropriate, they were located in places that could be defended, such as hilltops.

HOUSING

Towns and cities generally had rich and poor neighborhoods, with houses ranging from simple shacks to vast mansions. The city of Teotihuacán, for example, was laid out in *barrios* —sectors belonging to different social groups, made up of walled compounds in which people lived. Near the heart of the city lay the palaces of the wealthy and important families, which consisted of large complexes of rooms lavishly decorated with wall-paintings. Other

compounds beyond them contained the workshops and homes of craftsmen. Some of these compounds housed

Towns were located at key places on trade routes

traders—some from Teotihuacán and others from foreign states like Monte Albán. On the edge of the city lived the farmers in tiny, cramped houses packed tightly together.

Similar contrasts were to be found in towns and cities all over the world —from the lavishly furnished villas of Roman cities like Pompeii, with their painted walls and fine gardens, to the cramped apartment blocks (*insulae*) where the poorer Romans lived. But the differences were not always so marked. In the cities of the Indus Valley civilization (around 3000–2000

▲ *Many early cities had houses with large gardens. This ancient Egyptian painting shows the owner of the house and his wife standing in their garden, which has a pool surrounded by trees and date palms. The house is built on a platform to put it above the level of the annual flood.*

B.C.), for example, although there were houses of various sizes, all were comfortable and provided with facilities such as bathrooms.

ROYAL PALACES

One dwelling often stood out from all the rest—that of the ruler. In some societies the chief priests were the leaders, their residences forming part of sacred complexes. Other societies were ruled by kings who resided in magnificent palaces like that of the Assyrian king Sennacherib, who built his "Palace without a Rival" in Nineveh.

As well as having finely furnished private apartments, palaces often included public halls for audiences and official meetings, and many offices and other administrative rooms, along with accommodation for a host of servants, plus kitchens, storerooms, and archives. Vast statues of winged bulls with human heads adorned Sennacherib's palace, and its walls were decorated with reliefs depicting the king's successful military campaigns.

OFFICIAL BUILDINGS

Sometimes there were also separate administrative buildings. For example, the forums, the centers of Roman towns and cities, included law courts, public records offices, and a building for the administrative assembly. In countries with a warm climate public business was often conducted out of doors—in Athens, for example, the

▶ *Ruins of the ancient city of Hattusas, the capital of the Hittite Empire (1700–1190 B.C.). The site chosen was a natural stronghold on a high, rocky ridge, where many streams flowed down the mountains. The city's builders made use of all the suitable land, as well as creating more flat ground by building terraces. Houses were built of mud bricks and stone. A stout wall encircled the city.*

WATER SUPPLY

For people living in ancient towns and cities a good water supply was essential. Water was important for drinking, cooking, washing people and clothes, and for sanitation. The quality of these amenities was very variable. The cities of the Indus Valley civilization had an excellent system of drains, servicing the bathrooms and latrines that were a feature of most houses. Wells in the houses provided the domestic water supply for many households, while others used wells set in the streets. The Greeks and Romans also had excellent public water systems. The Greeks provided running water in fountain-houses from which people could fetch water for use at home or could take a shower. The Romans' water system supplied public fountains, baths, and latrines—which often seated large numbers of people—and also included carefully planned sanitation pipes to remove waste.

assembly of all male citizens took place on a hill overlooking the Agora, the heart of the city. Law courts might be accompanied by prisons and places of punishment and execution. In Aztec towns the market included a building where the market judges sat to hear cases and administer the law.

The Roman Forum and Athenian Agora also contained temples. Major religious structures were often at the center of ancient towns and cities. They took many forms but were often impressive mounds—high-stepped pyramids topped by soaring temples in Mesoamerica, ziggurats in Mesopotamia, *stupas* in southern Asia. Much of the Sri Lankan capital, Anuradhapura, for example, was taken up by Buddhist monasteries, each focused on a *stupa*

◀ *The ruins of the city of Teotihuacán, in modern Mexico, which flourished around 200–600 A.D. The city was laid out on a grid pattern with a wide avenue running through the center called the Street of the Dead. At the far end of the avenue stands the Pyramid of the Moon, which originally had a temple on the top.*

as its center of worship. In contrast, the shrines in Celtic *oppida* (pre-Roman towns) were often simple enclosures containing deep sacrificial pits or displays of severed heads.

LEISURE FACILITIES

Many Mesoamerican towns and cities also included a court for playing the sacred ballgame—sometimes with a rack containing the skulls of defeated players. Equally grim was the Roman amphitheater, where criminals were executed, wild beasts slaughtered, and gladiators fought to the death.

But not all public entertainment was violent. The Romans also provided public baths as a place for people to meet, relax, and wash. Greek cities had gymnasia where men exercised and practiced various sports, and theaters for cultural entertainment. In some Indian cities gaming boards were carved in public places so people could play.

Public parks and recreational water also featured in many southern Asian cities. Anuradhapura, for example, was richly provided with tanks (pools) for bathing, supplied with water from a clever system of canals and reservoirs. Canals also supplied water for royal parks and private gardens in the Assyrian city of Nineveh. Here, as in other Mesopotamian cities, parks were maintained so that the king could hunt

---

Canals supplied water for royal parks and private gardens

---

game, particularly lions. Many of the houses of wealthy Egyptians also had private gardens, often with ponds.

Craftsmen usually lived in a town or city. In some societies, such as early

▲ *This street scene is a 19th-century artist's impression of how the Roman city of Pompeii looked before it was destroyed by a volcanic eruption in 79 A.D. In the center is the Temple of Fortuna Augusta, which, like other public buildings, was painted and brightly decorated with murals and sculpture.*

▲ *The Forum Baths in the Roman city of Pompeii as they are today. The caldarium was the second hottest room in the baths. It had a hot, steamy atmosphere like a modern sauna and a pool where people could bathe.*

from the distant oceans—and from the nearby countryside—the wool of local sheep and reeds from rivers. Some crafts could be practiced in the home, such as spinning and weaving; others, like metalworking, required specialized premises, often in a distinct area of the town. Forges were often sited on the outskirts of cities because of the smells, noise, and general level of pollution produced.

The wealth of towns and cities made them vulnerable to attack

Towns and cities were bases for merchants, who organized and led expeditions to carry locally produced raw materials and goods to distant lands. Towns also accommodated foreign traders, often in special quarters, such as the Assyrian *karum* in the Anatolian town of Kanesh.

The prosperity of towns and cities made them a focus for enemy attack, so it was rare for them to be undefended. Early Roman settlements in Britain, for example, were fortresses to subdue the hostile natives. They were eventually replaced by unwalled towns, except in areas where resistance continued. By the third century A.D., however, barbarians were threatening the peace, so defensive walls with massive gates were built.

Mesopotamia, craftsmen were employed by the temple authorities or as part of the royal household to produce the goods (such as woolen textiles and pottery) required for everyday use and for trade. In others, such as Greece or Aztec Mesoamerica, craftsmen made goods to sell in markets or shops.

Often both systems operated, some craftsmen working exclusively for noble patrons, while others depended on selling their wares to the public, as in Han China (202 B.C–220 A.D.). As the home of kings, nobles, and priests, and many other people, towns and cities were the best place for craft producers to work and live.

TRADE NETWORKS
Trading networks, too, were generally based on towns and cities. The raw materials needed by craftspeople were brought both from far afield—metal ores and precious stones from remote mines, timber from faraway hills, shells

SEE ALSO:

◆ ÇATAL HÖYÜK
◆ MONTE ALBÁN
◆ POMPEII
◆ ROME
◆ TEOTIHUACÁN

TRADE

920

Trade is the process of exchanging or buying and selling goods. If a civilization did not have or could not make the goods people required, it needed to get them from somewhere else. As members of a society traveled—conquering or exploring—they came across exotic goods and brought them back home. Traders then set out on organized expeditions to bring back more of these goods in exchange for food and manufactured products.

People certainly traded goods before there were written records, but it is impossible to say exactly when this first happened. Archaeological finds show that early humans treasured exotic objects, such as shells and curiously shaped stones, but whether they were collected by individuals during their travels, obtained by exchanging gifts, or traded is uncertain.

One of the first materials known to have been traded was obsidian (black volcanic glass). Obsidian was prized in many parts of the world, such as Mesoamerica and the Mediterranean,

▲ *This Egyptian tomb painting from 1550-1295 B.C. shows a jewelry-making workshop. Egypt was known for its fine jewelry, enamel work, and carved ivory, which were traded for foreign goods such as silver and timber.*

◄ *The dark, glassy volcanic rock called obsidian was one of the first items to be traded by early peoples. This knife was made by the Hopewell people of Ohio using obsidian that came from the Rocky Mountains, over 1,000 miles (1,600km) away.*

▼ *This sixth-century B.C. Greek vase shows merchants weighing bales of cloth. Woolen cloth was one of ancient Greece's main exports.*

because it could be made into tools of exceptional sharpness, and also because it had an attractive shiny appearance. It is only found in a few places (near volcanoes), and scientific tests are able to determine where a particular piece of obsidian or an obsidian tool came from. This makes it possible to trace the patterns of trade in obsidian.

EXCHANGE NETWORKS

In this early form of trading, obsidian was picked up or quarried by people living near its sources. They passed some of it to neighboring groups, who then passed some on to their neighbors. Through many such small steps obsidian might eventually end up as far as 1,000 miles (1600km) from its source. Other exotic materials, such as shells and nodules of pure copper, were also distributed in this way. It is likely that they were passed as gifts between relatives in nearby settlements.

In Australia gift-exchange networks carried seashells inland and brought stone for making tools from inland quarries toward the coast. As materials moved farther from their source, they became rarer and almost certainly more valuable.

MESOPOTAMIA

Around 6000 B.C. people began to settle and farm on the highly fertile plains of the Tigris and Euphrates rivers in Mesopotamia. On the mud of this fertile plain they were able to raise abundant crops and keep many sheep, goats, and other animals that provided them not only with meat but also wool and skins. It is sometimes said that mud was the only raw material that they had—it could also be made into pottery or molded into bricks for constructing houses and temples.

But mud could not provide all that people needed—early Mesopotamians also needed timber for many purposes

▶ *A seventh-century B.C. stone relief carving of two merchants from the Assyrian city of Carchemish. The city was located near the place where caravans trading between Anatolia and Mesopotamia crossed the Euphrates River. This meant that it became a prosperous and important trading center.*

and stone and metal ore for making tools. To embellish their temples and demonstrate the importance of their kings and nobles, they also wanted precious materials, such as gold and lapis lazuli (a beautiful semiprecious blue stone). So the Mesopotamians set out on trading expeditions to obtain the materials they required in exchange for their surplus food and manufactured goods, such as pottery vessels, stone carvings, and woolen cloth.

Unlike earlier exchange networks, which probably continued to operate, this trade was between peoples living a great distance apart, and it did not necessarily involve the people living in the areas between them. There could still, however, be a number of stages in the trade—lapis lazuli from Badakshan (in modern Afghanistan) was carried to trading towns on the Iranian plateau, such as Shahr-i Sokhta and Tepe Yahya, which traded it on to other local towns and then to the cities of Sumer. The people involved in these exchanges were not related, and so each group tried to get the best bargain possible.

MESOAMERICA

This pattern was broadly repeated in many parts of the world. In Mesoamerica gift exchange continued for a long period of time. It included an exchange of cultivated plants that helped farming develop across the region as plants from one area became established in others. By the time of the Olmecs, around 1200 B.C., this somewhat haphazard arrangement was giving way to a more organized system.

The Olmecs established far-flung trading outposts in areas that produced valuable materials such as jade. Many of the goods that were exchanged between Mesoamerican communities

▼ *This 19th-century picture of a Greek harbor shows a merchant ship being unloaded. The incoming cargo probably included sacks of foodstuffs, while the pots in the foreground are about to be loaded. Greek pots like these, called amphorae, were used all over the Mediterranean region for transporting wine and oil.*

were essential items for religious rituals—incense, conch shells for horns, stingray spines and obsidian blades for bloodletting, jade for ritual masks, and iron ore for mirrors.

STATE CONTROL

At first the priests and rulers (in some regions they were the same people) organized this trade. They employed craftspeople, who made goods, and they accumulated surplus agricultural produce as taxes or offerings. They issued these commodities to merchants who traded them with people in other lands. The goods and materials they received in exchange were returned to the temple or palace treasury and were then distributed to members of the community in return for services, or used for the glorification of the leaders, or to pay for various public works.

UNDERWATER EVIDENCE

Shipwrecks provide dramatic evidence of trade in action. In the 14th century B.C., for example, a merchant ship was wrecked off the coast of Anatolia (modern Turkey) near Kas. It was discovered by a sponge diver in 1982. The ship's home port may have been one of the Canaanite cities on the east Mediterranean coast between Anatolia and Egypt, where it was loaded with cedar wood, amphorae (large pottery jars) containing yellow terebinth resin (burned as incense or used in making a highly prized perfume), and blue glass ingots. The ship sailed from there to Ugarit (in modern Syria) before heading for Cyprus, where it took on board copper ingots and Cypriot pottery. From there it would probably have called at Hittite ports in Anatolia on the way to Crete and Egypt had it not sunk. Its cargo also included Mycenaean pottery, ingots of tin, timber from North Africa, amber from the Baltic, ivory, and ostrich eggshells, as well as the crew's food supply, which included fruits, nuts, wheat, and barley.

But even in early times the state probably did not completely control trade. Mesopotamian merchants sent on official trading missions were allowed to do some private trading as well. In time private trading increased, and much of it took place in markets.

Although there was probably a great deal of bargaining, some commodities began to be used as a regular medium of exchange. In the Middle East silver was used to pay for goods, and societies as far apart as Egypt and China used certain types of seashell. Having an

agreed method of payment made trading exchanges much simpler. The invention of coins made trading even easier. The first coins were probably made in Lydia, a city-state in western Asia, before 635 B.C. The idea was soon taken up by Lydia's neighbors, the Greeks and Persians. Almost at the same time, coinage also appeared in India and China. Coinage, however, required a certain level of organization and did not become universal.

TRADE RECORDS

Trading required a great deal of record-keeping. Many of these records have survived, giving us a good idea of trade within many communities. One of the best sets of records details the trade in the 19th and 18th centuries B.C. between Anatolia and the prosperous Assyrian city of Ashur.

Family firms of Assyrian merchants established trading stations (called *karum*) in Anatolian towns, particularly in Kanesh (modern Kultepe in Turkey), where more than 10,000 clay tablets giving details of their business have been found. Using donkeys to transport their goods, the Assyrians brought textiles and a metal (probably tin) to Anatolia and in exchange took back gold and silver.

A tax of 1/120 of the value of their goods was paid by the merchants to the authorities in Ashur as they left and a tax of 2/65 to the ruler in Kanesh on arrival. Usually the head of the family firm operated the Ashur end of the business, while junior family members ran the *karum* branches. The same merchants were also involved in trade with more distant lands.

Many trade items were transported by water—seas, rivers, and canals —because it was much easier than transporting goods overland. Boats could carry large, heavy goods—like blocks of quarried stone for building

▼ *A modern-day market in Tunisia. Markets like this brought ancient peoples together and provided an opportunity not only for trading goods but also for exchanging news and ideas.*

—that would be difficult and very expensive to transport by land. Land transport was only used where water transport was not possible. Although some societies, such as the Romans, the Incas, and the Pueblo people of the American Southwest, built fine roads, they were the exception. Most land transport had to cope with problems like dense vegetation, rugged surfaces, mountains, and rivers.

TRANSPORT METHODS

Some societies used pack animals, such as the donkeys of the early Assyrian traders, the llamas of South America, and the camels that made it possible to ply trade routes across the Sahara and Arabian Deserts. However, where suitable animals were not available,

▲ *A caravan of camels in Africa. Because camels can travel long distances without water, they were invaluable for transporting goods on long-distance trade routes, such as the Silk Road, which crossed deserts.*

people had to carry goods themselves. After the wheel was invented, bullocks, horses, onagers (semiwild asses), camels, and even dogs could be used to pull carts and wagons.

TRADE ROUTES

As trade routes developed, they became an important means of communication. News traveled along trade routes as traders exchanged information. Trade routes were also a means of cultural exchange. Envoys could travel with merchants to distant countries and bring back reports of how other societies lived. One such

"foreign correspondent" was the Chinese envoy who visited Angkor Wat in the 13th century A.D. He recorded his impressions and took back home reports of a rich city with a lavishly decorated palace and a king who rode out on an elephant with golden tusks.

One of the most famous overland trade routes was the Silk Road. The rapid growth of Asian cities in the first millennium B.C. stimulated the growth of trade across Asia. The Silk Road crossed the steppes and deserts of Central Asia, connecting China with the Middle East and bringing Asian goods to Europe. The dangers, huge distances, and difficult terrain meant that few traders traveled the whole route. Instead, caravan routes linked together towns, which grew wealthy through their control of the trade.

A VOICE FROM THE PAST

This is how a Spanish friar described the way of life of an Aztec merchant:

❝ [He is forever] buying and selling, traveling to all the markets in the land, bartering cloth for jewels, jewels for feathers, feathers for stones, and stones for slaves, always dealing in goods of great importance and great value. [These merchants] enhance their social position with their wealth. ❞

SEE ALSO:

◆ AFRICA
◆ MESOPOTAMIA
◆ MONEY AND WEALTH
◆ TITHES AND TAXES
◆ TRANSPORTATION

TRANSPORTATION

For tens of thousands of years walking and running were the only means of transportation open to people. However, as the first civilizations began to emerge, people began to develop new means of getting around. Using boats to travel on rivers, riding horses, and inventing the wheel meant that people could cover distances more quickly and more easily. These developments also allowed people to transport goods from place to place and thus opened up the possibility of long-distance trade.

The first vehicles of transport to be developed were the log raft on water and the sled on land. Water transport was probably the first advance beyond walking as people took advantage of the currents of rivers and seas. We do not know when the first boats were built, but people probably started floating on logs many thousands of years ago. For example, it is clear that some sort of watercraft, if only a form of log raft, was necessary for people to cross the water barrier that separated Australia from the Asian continent 40,000 or more years ago. By 8,000 years ago dugout canoes were being used in Europe and North America. One

▲ *This relief from the palace of Sargon II shows Assyrian ships carrying imported cargoes of cedar wood. The development of oceangoing boats allowed ancient peoples to build up large trading networks.*

dugout canoe from this period was found at Tybrind Vig in Denmark. It was 30 ft (9.5m) long and could carry six to eight people.

Larger sailing boats have been in use since at least 4000 B.C. The ancient Egyptians used such vessels to transport stone obelisks and other bulky goods up and down the Nile River. As well as sails, these ships also featured rows of oars, so that they could still travel when winds and currents were unfavorable. The Egyptians soon started to sail in the open waters of the Mediterranean and to trade with nearby islands such as Crete. The Phoenicians were another ancient people who quickly mastered the techniques of sailing in the open sea. Between around 1100 and 800 B.C. they used their knowledge to develop extensive trading networks, traveling as far as Cornwall in the British Isles.

TRAVELING ON LAND

The first land vehicles were probably the sleds used by migrating hunter-gatherers in snowy areas. They used these sleds to pull their belongings along as they walked. At Vis in Russia archaeologists have found fragments of skis that are about 7,000 years old.

It was not until the invention of the wheel that truly practical vehicles arrived. The wheel was invented around 6,000 years ago in the Middle East and Europe, about the same time that people discovered that animals, especially cattle, could be used to pull heavy things. Plows and wagons are two developments of this period. The earliest wagons were probably used very close to settlements for hauling crops, timber, firewood, and animal carcasses. Between settlements paths were probably so uneven that it would have been quicker to walk.

It is important to realize that the use of the wheel in ancient times was

▼ *One of the first vehicles of transport to be used by human beings was the dugout canoe, made from a single log. Modern versions like this one from Ecuador are still used today.*

restricted to a relatively limited part of the world. Wheeled vehicles were unknown in the Americas and in Africa south of the Sahara Desert. Even in Egypt and China such vehicles appeared only after about 2000 B.C.

The domestication of the horse before 3000 B.C. on the steppes of southern Russia led eventually to new possibilities for animal-drawn transport. Around 2000 B.C. horse-drawn wagons came into wider use, and two-wheeled vehicles called chariots were developed for warfare, especially on the open

RIDING HORSES

The first people to domesticate the horse and use it for transportation were the nomadic tribes who lived in the steppes of Central Asia. It is estimated that these people first rode horses some time around 3500 B.C. Horseriding quickly spread to western Asia—the Assyrians, Hittites, and Babylonians all hunted and fought on horseback.

Saddles first developed in the steppe region and were used by the Scythians—an extremely warlike, nomadic steppe people—from around 400 B.C. We know this because perfectly preserved leather saddles have been found in the graves of Scythian chieftains. In fact, nearly all the pieces of equipment used by modern riders were first developed by the people of the steppes. One exception is the stirrup, which was first used by the Chinese in around 400 A.D. However, it was quickly adopted by the nomads, and it was they who introduced it to Europe and western Asia.

▲ *A 19th-century illustration of steppe dwellers with their horses.*
Horses helped the nomadic steppe people move around easily.

plains of Mesopotamia. Improvements in wheel design, including the use of spokes, led to the adoption of light and fast chariots for personal transportation and for fighting in southeastern Europe, the Middle East, and Egypt.

Animals were not only used to pull chariots and wagons. On the open steppes of southern Russia and Asia horseriding became the standard means of personal transportation among nomadic peoples. Across the deserts of northern Africa, Central Asia, Iran, and the Arabian Peninsula camels came into use as pack animals after people started keeping them

about 2500 B.C. Because camels could tolerate dry regions and travel long distances without water they were an ideal means of transportation on trade routes that spanned these deserts. In the Andes Mountains of South America llamas and alpacas were domesticated and were also used for transport.

ROADS AND PATHS

The harnessing of animal power for transportation by ancient peoples did not solve one fundamental problem. How could these animals, the vehicles they pulled, and their riders travel over rough or forested terrain and cross swamps and marshes? Rivers posed yet another problem, and they could be crossed only at shallow points or with the help of boats. But even on land the new opportunities provided by animals and vehicles would have been very limited unless something was done to provide smooth tracks for people to walk on.

The world's first roads were the footpaths that were worn down by people walking along commonly used trails. Such paths have long since disappeared. The first roads that we can identify archaeologically are the wooden walkways that were built by the people of northern Europe to cross swamps. One such walkway was found in southwestern England. Now known as Sweet Track, it was built to cross a large marsh and was about one mile (1.6km) long. Studies of the rings in

▲ This bronze Chinese model of a horse and chariot dates back to the second century B.C. Only the very rich could afford to travel in this way, so the figure in the chariot probably represents an important court official.

27

ROADS ACROSS THE ANDES

By the time of the arrival of the Spanish in 1532 A.D. the Inca Empire stretched for 2,500 miles (4,000km) along the west coast of South America. A highway system with about 25,000 miles (40,000km) of roads enabled pedestrians and llama caravans to get anywhere in the empire. Since they were not designed for wheeled traffic, Inca roads could surmount remarkable obstacles. Long flights of steps were used to scale steep slopes. In mountainous areas the roads could get as narrow as 3 ft (1m) wide, although they were more commonly 15 ft (4.5m) wide in flat terrain and sometimes 35 ft (10m) across as they approached cities. Retaining walls and drainage ditches prevented the roads from being closed due to natural disasters such as rockslides and washouts.

Perhaps the most remarkable engineering feats of the Inca roadbuilders, however, were their bridges, including the world's first suspension bridges. Over the Apurimac River they built a suspension bridge that was 150 ft (45m) long. Three thick ropes formed the floor of the bridge, and two more formed a hand-rail either side. Although they were sturdy, such bridges must have been scary to cross as they swayed in the wind and sagged under the weight of people and llamas.

▲ *The Inca road leading from the town of Machu Picchu to the empire's capital at Cuzco is still clearly visible after 500 years.*

the timbers from which it was built have dated the walkway's construction precisely to the winter of 3807–06 B.C.

One of the earliest major paved roads was the Persian Royal Road. During the time of the Achaemenid dynasty (559–330 B.C.) the road led from the empire's capital of Susa near the Persian Gulf right to Sardis in Lydia (modern Turkey), a distance of some 1,550 miles (2,500km). The road evolved gradually from ancient trading routes that were probably in use from the fourth millennium B.C.

The greatest road-builders of the ancient world were the Romans. Like

▲ *One of the most famous of all Roman roads, the Appian Way led south from Rome, stretching 410 miles (660km) to Hydruntum in the southeast corner of Italy.*

all ancient empires, the Roman empire needed good roads to connect its capital to outlying areas. Roman emperors had to be able to supply and reinforce their armies at short notice, while the empire's administrators needed to be able to move easily back and forth from the capital to the provinces. A vast quantity of goods and products, meanwhile, had to be transported back from the outer reaches of the empire to Rome itself.

The Romans began their road network to connect their settlements in Italy. Their first, and most famous, stone-paved road was the Via Appia, or Appian Way, which runs south from Rome and is still in use today. The paving of roads was a significant

advance, since it meant that in wet weather vehicles could still use them without getting stuck in mud. As the Roman Empire grew, the Roman road system expanded. By 50 A.D. it reached from the Atlantic Ocean in the west to the Euphrates River in the east.

Although the Romans left no map of their roads, enough of them survive today to permit this network to be traced. The Romans also set up milestones along their roads that recorded distance and the dates of construction and repair. Inns and horse-changing posts were established at intervals to serve the travelers.

CANALS

The earliest canals were built in Mesopotamia in around 5000 B.C. in order to irrigate fields. However, water channels could also be used for transportation, and in time many began to serve both purposes. One of the most impressive canals constructed in the ancient world was built by the Persian king Darius in around 500 B.C. It connected the Mediterranean and Red seas and followed much of the same route as the modern Suez Canal.

The ancient Chinese also built many large-scale transport canals. In the seventh century A.D. a 600-mile (960km) canal was constructed to help transport rice from the delta of the Yangtze River to distant cities. It was constantly rebuilt and lengthened, and forms the basis of a water transport system that is still in use today.

SEE ALSO:

◆ **ANIMALS**
◆ **INCAS**
◆ **NAVIGATION**
◆ **STEPPE NOMADS**
◆ **TRADE**

TROY

Greek legend told of a city called Troy that was defended by mighty walls and towers. In his epic poem the *Iliad* the Greek poet Homer wrote about the Trojan War, fought between the Greeks and the Trojans. But after its people lost the war, the great city of Troy apparently disappeared without trace, and by the 19th century most historians believed that it had only really existed in ancient myth. However, the German archaeologist Heinrich Schliemann (1822–90) was to prove the doubters wrong.

When he was just seven years old, Schliemann saw an artist's impression in a history book of how Troy might

have looked, and it convinced him that the city really had existed and that its ruins must lie somewhere. Years later, Schliemann's studies of Homer's poem led him to the Aegean coast of western Anatolia and a hill called Hissarlik in modern-day Turkey. A few other archaeologists had already suggested this as a possible site for Troy, and when he got there, Schliemann felt sure that they were right.

In 1870 Schliemann started digging at Hissarlik and soon found, 15ft (4.5m) beneath the surface soil, an ancient wall of huge stones. A year later he returned and made more finds. By 1872 Schliemann had more than 100 local workmen helping him. They found the remains of not just one ancient city but several cities built one on top of the other. It was clear that as

▲ *The remains of the city walls of Troy VI, which flourished between around 2000 and 1350 B.C. Historians believe that this version of the city was destroyed by an earthquake.*

each city had been destroyed, another had been built on the ruins. The diggers found more walls, urns, and fragments of pottery. But was this Troy? In June 1873 Schliemann found what he thought was the answer.

THE TREASURES OF PRIAM

At the bottom of a wall that he was excavating, Schliemann saw a gleaming piece of gold. When he took the piece out, he found that it was a gold diadem. Shortly afterward, he found another diadem, gold bracelets, a gold goblet, and a large silver container with thousands of small gold rings. Schliemann was overjoyed, convinced that he had found the treasure of Priam, the legendary last king of Troy.

After Heinrich Schliemann's death, excavations at Troy were carried on by his colleague Wilhelm Dörpfeld and later by archaeologists from the University of Cincinnati. They found that the gold that Schliemann called "Priam's treasure" was actually from a period about 1,000 years before King Priam and the Trojan War. It came from the second of the nine cities that lay one on top of the other.

Troy was probably founded in the early Bronze Age, which began about

3000 B.C. in Anatolia. Over the following centuries Troy became an extremely important trading center, mainly thanks to its location. Troy lay not only on a major land route between Asia and Europe but also on the sea route between the Aegean and the Black Sea. Because of this Troy became extremely wealthy, and historians believe that it served as the capital of

▲ *Troy was well placed to trade with the cities of ancient Greece.*

◀ *Excavation work being carried out at Troy. This contemporary illustration shows workmen uncovering the Temple of Athena, part of Troy IX.*

THE TROJAN WAR

According to legend and the works of Homer, the Trojan War began when Paris, the son of King Priam of Troy, stole the wife of Menelaus, king of Sparta. Her name was Helen, and she was the most beautiful woman in the world. Menelaus's brother, Agamemnon, organized a huge army carried by a fleet of 1,000 ships to win Helen back.

Greek soldiers laid siege to Troy for 10 years, but they could not conquer the walled city. Then Odysseus, one of the Greek commanders, thought up a cunning plan. The Greeks built a huge wooden horse and placed it outside the walls of Troy, and then they sailed away. The Trojans thought the horse was a sacred offering and took it into their city. But the wooden horse was actually full of Greek warriors who crept out of the horse at night and opened the city gates for the rest of their army, which had sailed back from a nearby island. The Greeks took Helen back, killed King Priam and the Trojan men, took the women captive, and burned Troy to the ground.

Some historians believe that the legend of the Trojan War is based on a number of battles that took place between 1500 and 1200 B.C. Others think there really was one great war that took place around 1250 B.C.

▲ *Greek soldiers climb out of their wooden horse and unlock the gates to the city of Troy.*

the surrounding region, an area that we now know as the Troas.

THE NINE CITIES OF TROY

Archaeologists divide the history of Troy into a series of distinct periods. The first Troy was a small fortified citadel to which local farmers and villagers moved in times of danger.

The second Troy, built on top of the first city and called Troy II by archaeologists, was a larger and wealthier city, and traded extensively with the Mycenaeans of Greece. This city came to an end through fire, which led Schliemann to mistake it for Homer's Troy. The next three citadels were each larger than the previous one.

▶ *Taken at the time of Schliemann's excavations, this photograph shows a collection of pottery storage jars found at Troy. They date back to the early Bronze Age and the city known to archaeologists as Troy II.*

Troy VI had many new settlers and was far more heavily influenced by the Mycenaeans than its predecessors. It was destroyed by an earthquake about 1300 B.C. The next city, which we now call Troy VIIa, was looted and burned around 1250 B.C. Archaeologists know this because they have been able to date imported Mycenaean pottery very accurately. Most historians believe that Troy VIIa was the legendary city of King Priam that featured in the story of the Trojan War. Its successor, Troy VIIb, did not last long. It was abandoned about 1100 B.C. and left unoccupied for several centuries..

A new chapter in the history of Troy began at the start of the seventh century B.C., when Greeks from the nearby island of Lemnos reoccupied it. The city now became known as Ilium and prospered for many years.

The Romans eventually sacked this city in 85 B.C. and built Troy IX, the final version of the city recognized by archaeologists. The Roman city was abandoned around 400 A.D., and Troy remained undisturbed until the day Heinrich Schliemann rediscovered it.

▶ *This earring is part of a hoard of golden jewelry known as Priam's Treasure. However, it actually dates back to around 2300 B.C., roughly 1,000 years before the Trojan War.*

SEE ALSO:

◆ **GREECE**
◆ **LITERATURE**
◆ **MYCENAEANS**
◆ **ORAL TRADITION**

TUTANKHAMUN'S TOMB

Most of the famous pharaohs of ancient Egypt earned immortality through their achievements as soldiers or builders, conquering territory or creating enormous temples and tombs. Tutankhamun was neither a great soldier nor a great builder, he only reigned for nine years, and he died before he was 20; yet he is probably the best known of all the pharaohs. This is because of the dramatic discovery of his tomb in 1922. Unlike all the other royal tombs, it had never been plundered by tomb robbers and so was full of the most magnificent treasures.

Tutankhamun was born about 1341 B.C. Although it is not known for certain who his parents were, the most likely candidates are Amenhotep IV (later known as Akhenaten) and his queen, Nefertiti. Given the name Tutankhaten, the child was brought up at the new royal capital of Akhetaten. Akhenaten had rejected the traditional gods of Egypt in favor of a new god, Aten, and moved his court from the old capital of Thebes. Unlike the old gods, Aten was not depicted as a person or animal but as the sun. Tutankhaten's close connection with the royal family is emphasized by his marriage to Akhenaten's daughter Ankhesenpaaten, who was much older than him and was probably his sister. This marriage would have made Tutankhaten's claim to the throne more secure.

When Akhenaten died, it seems that Tutankhaten's brother Smenkhkare became pharaoh for a very brief time before Tutankhaten, aged about nine, succeeded him. His name was changed to Tutankhamun, and Akhetaten was abandoned. The removal of the royal court to Memphis and Amun's reinstatement as the chief god of Egypt indicates that the young king's advisers

▲ *This detail from the back of Tutankhamun's golden throne shows the king and his wife Ankhesenpaaten. The couple wear elaborate jeweled crowns.*

▶ *An artist's impression of the discovery of Tutankhamun's tomb. A worker peers through the doorway separating the Antechamber from the Burial Chamber. The doorway is guarded by two life-size statues of the king.*

were against his father's ideas and wanted to restore the old ways.

Tutankhamun died aged about 18. Whether this was the result of a plot against him is unknown, but his body bears no unusual signs of violence. His death was certainly unexpected, since no tomb had yet been prepared for him in the Valley of the Kings. Instead, a small nonroyal tomb—perhaps intended for a favored courtier—was hastily pressed into service and quickly decorated during the 70 days required

for embalming the body. The modest nature of the tomb meant that unlike some of the larger, more magnificent tombs in the Valley of the Kings, the tomb of Tutankhamun was ignored and then forgotten, especially after the rubble waste from the nearby tomb of Ramses VI was dumped on top of it.

DISCOVERING THE TOMB

In 1922 Tutankhamun's rest of over 3,500 years came to an end when his tomb was discovered by the English archaeologist Howard Carter. Carter, sponsored by the aristocrat Lord Carnarvon, had been working in the Valley of the Kings since 1915. On November 4, 1922, workmen discovered a set of stone steps leading to a blocked doorway. The seals on the doorway were intact and named the owner—Tutankhamun. Beyond this sealed door a corridor led to a second door. Carter cut a small hole in it to see what lay ahead. What he saw was, in his own words, "everywhere the glint of gold." He was looking into the first of four rooms that, although small, were absolutely full of treasure.

▶ *Tutankhamun was brought up in Akhetaten. However, during his reign the site of the royal capital moved to the ancient city of Memphis.*

Mediterranean Sea

● **Memphis**

EGYPT

● **Akhetaten**

Nile River

Red Sea

● **Thebes**

▶ *The famous funeral mask of Tutankhamun. Made out of solid gold and decorated with glass and lapis lazuli, the mask has become the most instantly recognizable artwork of the ancient world.*

The first room, or Antechamber, measured 25.7 x 11.6 ft (7.8 x 3.5m). The most noticeable items in this room were three gilded ritual couches in the form of sacred animals stacked against the rear wall and, to the left of the doorway, a tangle of six dismantled chariots. Two further doorways led out of the Antechamber. The first led to a small room called the Annex, which seems to have been where the dead king's food, wine, and oils were stored. The other doorway was completely blocked and was guarded by a pair

A ROYAL COFFIN

The body of Tutankhamun was hidden by many protective layers. A huge shrine of wood covered with hammered gold and inscribed with writing nearly filled the chamber. Nesting within that, like the layers of a Russian doll, were three similar shrines. Within them was a sarcophagus (stone coffin) made of quartzite with a granite lid. When Howard Carter lifted the lid of the sarcophagus, he knew that he had discovered the undisturbed burial of a king.

Inside there was a wooden coffin of cypress wood covered with a thin layer of gold. Inside was a second coffin of gilded wood elaborately decorated with a range of precious materials, including faience, obsidian, and lapis lazuli. Finally, there was a coffin of solid gold that weighed 243 lb. (110kg). When the lid of this was lifted, it revealed the king's mummified body and a further surprise—the funeral mask of solid gold, lapis lazuli, and blue glass, which has become for many the most famous symbol of ancient Egypt. The king's hands were also covered with gold, and the mummy wrappings contained huge quantities of jewelry.

▼ *This pendant was found in Tutankhamun's tomb and is made of gold and a variety of precious stones. It bears the image of the scarab beetle, an animal sacred to the Egyptians.*

of life-size wooden statues of the king. This doorway led to the greatest prize of all—the Burial Chamber.

The Burial Chamber was also small for a king—20.9 x 13 ft (6.37 x 4.02m). It was the only room in the tomb to have painted decoration on its walls. More importantly, it was here that Tutankhamun himself lay.

Beyond the Burial Chamber was yet another small chamber. It was called the Treasury mainly because of the superb quality of the objects found within it, which included model boats, gold shrines, and jewel cases. Also in the Treasury were two miniature coffins, each containing a mummified fetus. Were these the stillborn children of the king, and was this why Tutankhamun did not leave even an infant heir to succeed him? The mystery may never be solved.

A RICH LEGACY

Sadly, Lord Carnarvon was never to know what lay inside the sarcophagus of Tutankhamun; he died in April 1923, and by then the lengthy task of emptying the tomb and conserving the objects that came from it had scarcely begun. The work was finally completed in 1932 by Carter, who died seven years later. Carnarvon and Carter's memorial is the wonderful collection of objects from the tomb of Tutankhamun and the story of what must be one of the most exciting and spectacular archaeological discoveries ever made.

SEE ALSO:

◆ **EGYPT**
◆ **JEWELRY**
◆ **TOMBS AND BURIAL RITES**

UR

In 1923 a British-American expedition was launched to excavate the ancient Sumerian city of Ur in southern Iraq. Standing close to the Euphrates River, Ur had flourished between 3000 and 2000 B.C. It was one of a number of city-states within the land of Sumer in ancient Mesopotamia. Although its buildings finally disappeared beneath the desert, Ur's name had been preserved because it was mentioned in the Bible as the birthplace of Abraham, one of the great early leaders of the Jewish people.

It was not until the early 20th century, however, that archaeologists knew for certain that Ur was located in Iraq. Clay tablets inscribed with writing had been found at a site known locally as Tell al-Muqayyar. When the tablets were deciphered, it was found that they referred to a king named Ur-Nammu, who was known to have become king of Ur in about 2112 B.C. So when the excavations began at al-Muqayyar, the archaeologists knew the site's ancient name. However, they had no idea of the treasures they would discover.

The leader of the expedition was a Briton named Sir Leonard Woolley, who was one of the most outstanding

▲ *The ruins of the city of Ur are dominated by the ziggurat, seen here in the background, which has been partly restored. Most buildings at Ur were built of mud brick, and the city was surrounded by a defensive wall.*

archaeologists of his time. Excavations at Ur occupied him for 12 years and were the high point of his career.

Working tirelessly with up to 400 local laborers, Woolley and his team began to uncover the remains of Ur. They soon unearthed floor plans of houses and temples, and rescued many everyday objects from the sand and dirt. They discovered that Ur's streets were narrow. Some had been laid out in a plan, others simply twisted around groups of small buildings. Houses were made of mud brick and built around a central courtyard. Floors were covered with reed mats. Furniture consisted mostly of low tables, stools, and chairs.

THE ROYAL CEMETERY

The most spectacular finds, however, were made in the royal cemetery. It contained more than 1,800 graves, most of them for the common people. But 17 of these graves were larger than the others and more sturdily built out of stone or brick. They also contained a wealth of precious objects made from gold and silver, often inlaid with gems. Only two of the 17 graves had escaped being plundered by tomb robbers in the past. But inscriptions of the names of kings were found, and this discovery convinced Woolley that they were the graves of Ur's royal rulers.

ROYAL TREASURES

The archaeologists used great care in the excavation. One of their techniques involved pouring paraffin wax over delicate objects to keep them from falling apart when lifted up. Soon marvellous objects, more than 4,500 years old, were being brought to light. They included statues, necklaces, beads, and women's headdresses decorated with wafer-thin gold shaped into leaves of willow and beech. There was also a helmet of hammered gold once worn by a king named Meskalamdu. It had

small holes drilled around the rim for fastenings that attached a cloth lining, traces of which were found inside.

Perhaps most fascinating of all the finds was a small wooden box that became known as the Standard of Ur. The box was inlaid with shell and a

▼ *This end of the wooden box called the Standard of Ur shows a goat being sacrificed to the gods.*

THE GREAT DEATH PIT

During his excavations Woolley found evidence that the people of Ur practiced a grim and apparently cruel burial ritual. It was clear from the skeletons found in the graves that when a king or queen died, their attendants were expected to accompany them into the afterlife. At a royal funeral these servants apparently followed the dead body of their ruler into the tomb. Then, having arranged themselves according to importance, they drank poison and lay down to die. It is unclear whether they did this voluntarily or whether they were executed.

The clearest evidence of this practice was found in the largest of Ur's tombs, which was found to have 74 skeletons, mostly of women. Called the Great Death Pit, the tomb measured about 25 sq. ft (2.3 sq. m). Woolley found that the victims had dressed up for their final moments. Gold ribbons were found among the bones, along with gold and lapis lazuli beads, and gold leaves from headdresses. There were also harps, decorated with silver and gold, mosaics, and two statues of rams made from wood overlaid with shell, gold, and lapis lazuli.

▼ This statue of a ram in a gold thicket was found in the Great Death Pit. The face and legs are gold, the horns, eyes, and fleece are lapis lazuli— all inlaid over wood.

blue stone called lapis lazuli, and may have been the sounding box of a lyre. What makes the box fascinating for scholars are the inlaid pictures on each of its long sides and the light they shed on Sumerian life. One of the two main panels shows a royal feast, while the other shows a war scene. The two end panels are also elaborately decorated. One of them shows a ram being sacrificed to the gods.

TRADING NETWORKS

Apart from the insight they give into Ur's burial rituals and the skill of its craftsmen, the finds show the city's trading patterns and partners. Lapis lazuli, for example, is known to have come from Afghanistan, which may have also provided tin. This metal was specially prized because when mixed with copper, it produces bronze. Shell came from the Persian Gulf. A red stone called carnelian was brought from what is now Iran. And timber was fetched from the Amanus Mountains in northwest Syria via the Euphrates River.

If Woolley was able to gather a lot of information from Ur's artifacts and burials, he gained even more from the collection of over 200 written records

▶ *This game board found at Ur is one of the most ancient known. Some experts think the game may have been the earliest form of backgammon, while others believe it could have been a race game.*

▼ *The city of Ur now lies in a desert, but in ancient times it was situated in a fertile plain much nearer to the Euphrates River, which has since changed its course.*

preserved on clay tablets. There were lists of animals and materials, such as fish, sheep, goats, and trees, as well as the names of individuals and their professions. They indicated that Ur had carpenters, metalsmiths, gardeners, cooks, and bricklayers. The tablets also described aspects of law. If a man wanted to divorce his wife, for example, he only had to pay a sum of money. Also, he was allowed to sell his children into slavery if he wanted to.

Ur's golden age lasted for about 100 years under the reigns of Ur-Nammu and his successors. This king was responsible for rebuilding the city's great temple—a stepped pyramid, or ziggurat. Although only its base remains, excavations showed that it was a solid structure made of brick. It rose up to 70 ft (21m) in three tiers, all connected by exterior staircases. On its summit was a small shrine where holy rituals took place. This ziggurat, like others in the region, was built to resemble a sacred mountain—a place where humans could stand closer to the gods. In the case of Ur the patron god was Nanna, god of the moon.

The end of Ur finally came in about 2000 B.C. A people called the Elamites invaded from the west and destroyed the city. Over the centuries it decayed and was totally covered by sand. Yet some 4,000 years later it was destined once again to see the light of day.

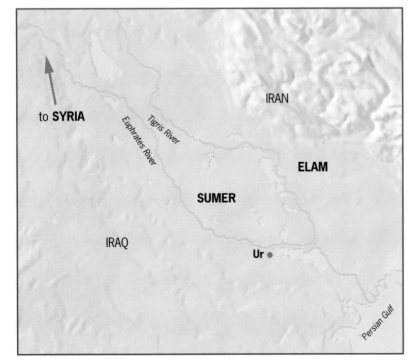

SEE ALSO:

◆ **ARCHAEOLOGY**
◆ **MESOPOTAMIA**
◆ **SUMERIANS**

VIKINGS

From the late eighth century A.D. the Vikings became known throughout Europe as bold, ruthless raiders. These fierce adventurers, also known as the Norsemen, sailed from their homeland in Scandinavia to terrorize a large area of western Europe. For over 400 years they made a succession of violent raids on coastal towns and villages, building up a fearsome reputation that has lived on to the present day.

The Vikings were the descendants of Germanic peoples who started moving to the northern region of Europe about 4,000 years ago. They settled in Scandinavia, a region that includes Denmark, Norway, and Sweden. By the end of the eighth century A.D. their population was growing quickly, and there may no longer have been enough good farmland at home to support their increasing numbers. This may have been the reason why they turned to raiding—and many young Vikings no doubt saw raiding as a quick and easy way of gaining wealth and honor.

Young Vikings saw raiding as an easy way of gaining wealth

Norwegian Vikings began their raids in the 790s, attacking the coasts of England, Ireland, and Scotland. The warriors usually appeared suddenly in a small group of ships, swarming ashore with their spears, swords, and battle axes. They plundered villages,

churches, and monasteries, and then just as quickly sailed away again. They were soon joined by Danish Vikings, who invaded England in 865. They conquered much of the country but were forced by King Alfred the Great to settle in the eastern region, which became known as the Danelaw.

By this time Norwegians and Danes had also looted and burned towns in France, Belgium, the Netherlands,

▲ *An artist's impression of a Viking longship with a raiding party about to land. Viking raids were greatly feared throughout northern Europe.*

▶ *The Vikings spread out from Scandinavia to colonize Britain, France, Russia, Iceland, and Greenland. Viking explorers are thought to have crossed the Atlantic as early as 1000 A.D. They probably landed at Baffin Island, although they may have sailed as far south as Labrador or even Maine.*

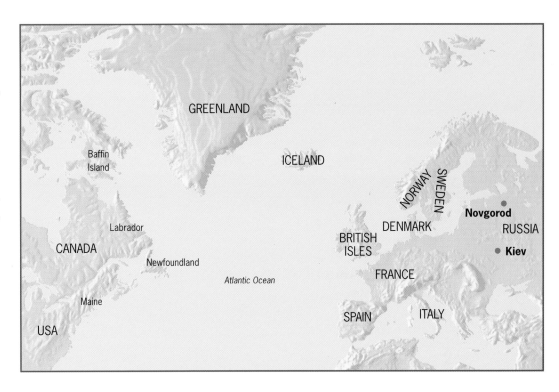

▼ *This buckle clasp from Norway is made of gold and inlaid with precious stones. The Vikings were expert metalworkers.*

Italy, and Spain, although they did not settle there permanently in any great numbers, as they had done in the British Isles.

However, Swedish Vikings did travel along the rivers of eastern Europe to set up trading centers, and by the late 800s the Slavic towns of Novgorod and Kiev were Viking strongholds. The main Viking people involved in these explorations were the Rus, and it is from them that we get the name of the modern country of Russia.

THE LONGSHIPS

In order to carry out their raids, the Vikings developed fast and sturdy warships. In ancient times the Scandinavians had used fragile canoes and boats made of animal skins stretched over a timber frame. Now, however, the Vikings built the powerful boats for which they became famous— their longships. These narrow boats were made from planks of oak rather than animal hide and had a steadying keel and a large central sail. A team of specialized craftsmen was needed to build each boat.

The Viking longship had up to 30 oars, each powered by one oarsman, on each side of the ship. They were used near land, when extra speed was needed, or when there was little wind. Each longship also had a single sail, made of tough woolen cloth strengthened by strips of leather, and it was generally used on the open sea. Viking ships could sail in shallow water, which made them useful for traveling along rivers and near coasts. They were also light enough to be hauled or carried over land when necessary.

VIKING EXPLORATIONS

Considering that they were expert navigators and sailors, it is not surprising that the Vikings were responsible for some of the greatest feats of exploration in the ancient world. In about 980 a Viking called Erik the Red was exiled from his home in Iceland and decided to sail west. He settled in an icy, inhospitable land that he named Greenland, hoping to encourage others to follow him. When his exile was over, he returned to Iceland and persuaded a group of adventurers to return with him and set up a large colony. The Viking settlements on Greenland lasted for several centuries.

Perhaps the greatest Viking explorer of them all was Erik's second son, Leif Eriksson, also known as Leif the Lucky. Sometime after 1000 he sailed west from Greenland across the Atlantic Ocean. He made landfall at a place he named Helluland, meaning "land of flat stones." It was probably Baffin Island in present-day Canada. The explorers then sailed on to Markland ("forest land"), which was probably the Canadian mainland of Labrador.

Finally, the Vikings reached Vinland ("wine land"), where wild grapes grew. This may have been the island of Newfoundland, where Viking remains have been found, though some historians believe that Vinland was in modern-day Maine. This great voyage of discovery took place nearly 400 years before Christopher Columbus crossed the Atlantic.

▶ *The remains of Brattahlid, the settlement that Erik the Red established in Greenland in the 10th century A.D. It was from Greenland that Erik's son, Leif Eriksson, crossed the Atlantic in one of the greatest voyages of discovery ever known.*

Modern archaeologists know a great deal about longships because the Vikings sometimes buried them with famous warriors.

Most Vikings were freemen, and many were farmers, growing cereals, fruit, and vegetables, and raising cattle, pigs, sheep, and goats. Merchants and others also made settlements near the coast, both at home in Scandinavia and when they traveled. Their wooden houses had roofs covered in turf. Early

▶ *A modern reconstruction of a Viking longhouse. A longhouse consisted of a single large communal room that housed several families living together. It was usually built from wood and the roof was thatched or covered with turf.*

towns had markets, where people traded furs, textiles, and iron. The freemen also traded in slaves, who were mainly prisoners who had been captured in raids. Slaves often worked as laborers and servants on farms and in workshops. They had few rights, and their children were born slaves as well.

Above the ordinary freemen and downtrodden slaves there was a class of Viking nobles. These nobles included those who had great wealth or those who were descended from honored warriors. The most powerful were chieftains who controlled large areas of countryside. About 890 Harold Finehair defeated many local kings and chieftains to become the first King of Norway.

ICELANDIC SETTLEMENTS

By the ninth century Norwegian Vikings had started settling in Iceland, where they led a more independent life and escaped the growing power of the king. Viking Iceland was a form of republic, where laws were passed by an assembly, called the *Althing*, which met on a rocky plain each midsummer. In other parts of the Viking world communities had a governing council called a *thing*. This council was made up only of freemen; women and slaves had no right to speak. The *thing* had such great power that it could even decide who should be king. It made laws, held trials to judge criminals, and decided whether the community should go to war.

The Vikings built different kinds of houses depending on the materials available in the region. Most were single-story structures, many with just one room, and the walls were mostly made of wood. There was usually one doorway and no windows, to keep in the heat from the hearth. The pitched roof was sometimes made of wooden tiles or thatch if reeds were available locally. The houses in Iceland and elsewhere had roofs made of a thick layer of turf.

VIKING GODS

The Vikings believed in many gods. The most important was Odin. He was king of all the Norse gods and goddesses, and was thought to live in a home of the gods called Asgard. He was the god of war and death, and he inspired ferocious Viking warriors called Berserkers, who worked themselves up into a frenzy of rage before throwing themselves into battle without armor.

Odin's oldest and most powerful son was red-bearded Thor, the god of thunder, lightning, and wind. He was the most popular Viking god because his supposed power over the weather had a great effect on people's daily lives. Thursday is named after Thor, and Friday after Frigg, his mother.

By the end of the 10th century contact with European Christians had led to the end of most of the earlier Norse beliefs. In about 960 King Harold Bluetooth of Denmark became a Christian, and soon after the colonists of Iceland voted to do the same.

▲ *This picture stone is believed to illustrate a story from Norse myth in which Odin, king of the gods, tricks the king Ermaneric into killing his son.*

In farming settlements there was often a large longhouse at the center, where a family and farmworkers all lived together. Inside the dark, smoky house there were wooden benches along the walls, where people sat during the day and slept at night. Women were in charge of the home and also of the farm if their husbands were away raiding or trading.

Over 300 years the Vikings had an enormous influence throughout Europe, and especially on England and France. Their last invasion of England took place in 1066, just weeks before it was conquered by the Normans, who themselves were descendants of Viking settlers in northern France. William the Conqueror, who became king of England after defeating King Harold at the Battle of Hastings, was a descendant of the Danish Viking chieftain Rollo, who had raided northern France and founded the Duchy of Normandy in 911.

The Vikings also had a lasting effect on Iceland, and this northern island still retains some elements of Viking culture today. In Scandinavia the three Viking kingdoms eventually became the modern-day nations of Denmark, Norway, and Sweden.

SEE ALSO:

◆ **ANGLO-SAXONS**
◆ **DECORATION**
◆ **EXPLORATION**
◆ **NAVIGATION**
◆ **SHIPS**

WARFARE AND WEAPONS

Wars are probably as old as the human race. Even in prehistoric times humans fought over food and land, using hunting tools such as sharpened flints and wooden sticks. Most early battles would have been ambushes or raids that relied on concealment and surprise. As armies became larger and more sophisticated, the role played by strategy (which means "the art of the general" in Greek) became increasingly important.

The first weapon to be designed specifically for war, around 10,000 B.C., was the club, or mace. A stone was attached to a wooden handle and used to crush the skull of an enemy. In the third millennium B.C. stone gave way to copper and then in about 2900 B.C. to bronze, making the mace much more effective. To counter the mace, men began to develop defensive armor, such as helmets. From then on warfare became a race between ever-more efficient ways of killing and improved methods of defense.

▲ *This ninth-century B.C. stone relief shows the Assyrian king Ashurnasirpal II besieging a city. The defenders were attacked with missiles and siege engines as soldiers scaled the walls.*

The mace, ax, poleax, stabbing spear, and sword were all shock weapons used in hand-to-hand combat. Equally important were missile weapons that were used to attack the enemy from afar. The simplest of them was the sling, which consisted of two thongs attached to a pouch that held a stone. The sling was whirled above the thrower's head to get maximum power before he let go of one thong and launched the stone. Gradually spears were developed that were specially designed for throwing and many civilizations, from the Aborigines to the Maya, invented devices for throwing a spear that gave it a greater range.

The mace head became more oval in shape so that a blow would be more concentrated and have a greater chance of penetrating a helmet. Gradually the mace evolved into the battle-ax and the poleax. The poleax was longer than an ax, and the blade was weighted with a metal ball. It took more strength to wield than the battle-ax, but its weight meant that it did a lot more damage to an enemy.

BATTLE-AX TO SWORD

The battle-ax was to be the most important cutting-edge hand weapon until around 1200 B.C., when the discovery of iron smelting meant that swords could be cast in iron. Although the design of the sword changed in different cultures and through the centuries, it remained an important weapon until the late 19th century A.D.

When first bronze and then iron-working developed, stabbing spears were one of the first weapons to be made from the new material. A further development of the stabbing spear was the pike—a long, metal-pointed spear with a heavy wooden shaft that could be as long as 10–20ft (3–6m).

▲ *Four swords from the late Bronze Age (about 1250–850 B.C.). Early copper and bronze swords had long, leaf-shaped blades and hilts (handles) that were an extension of the blade in handle form. By Roman times the hilt had become distinct from the short, flat blade. Swords did not become a truly effective weapon until they were forged in iron.*

Missile weapons were used to attack the enemy from afar

The most important missile weapon was the bow. Although the appearance of the bow altered very little from 10,000 B.C. onward, two technical developments vastly improved its range and penetration power. Around 3000 B.C. a composite bow made of wood, animal sinew, and horn provided more tension when the string was pulled back and propelled the arrow forward with great force. Around the sixth century B.C. the Chinese invented the crossbow, which had a mechanical winding mechanism and trigger. By the second century B.C. the crossbow was the main weapon of the Chinese army, but the design did not reach the West until the 12th century A.D.

TYPES OF ARMOR

The earliest armor known is depicted on a third millennium B.C. box called the Standard of Ur. It shows Sumerian soldiers wearing leather helmets and tunics. In about 2500 B.C. metal helmets were being made by the Sumerians. The earliest body armor known was found in a Mycenaean tomb dating from the late 15th century B.C. It was made of overlapping bronze plates, which would have provided excellent protection but also would have been very heavy. Lighter, more flexible armor was invented by the Egyptians and the Chinese around 1400 B.C., when small bronze plates were attached to leather clothing. The Assyrians were the first to use small iron plates instead of bronze.

Flexible mail armor made from small overlapping or linked iron pieces seems to have appeared in the third century B.C. in Greece and China, and may also have been used by the nomadic Scythians of southern Russia. The Aztec and Mayan soldiers of Mesoamerica wore thick, quilted cotton clothing, which was surprisingly effective because of its complicated, layered construction.

HORSES

In about 3500 B.C. steppe nomads started riding horses. Riding horseback gave warriors speed and mobility, but it was difficult to fight effectively on

horseback. Without saddles and stirrups warriors did not have much stability. This meant that they could not swing heavy weapons and could easily be pulled from their horses.

By 1850 B.C. steppe nomads were using horses to pull light two-wheeled carts. Once this invention reached other ancient peoples such as the Egyptians, the Hittites, and the Macedonians, it made a huge impact on warfare because warriors could now fight from a stable platform. Armies with chariots enjoyed military superiority for about five centuries. However, technical advances such as better saddles gradually enabled men to fight effectively on horseback. By the time of the Greek general

▲ *A stone relief from the seventh century B.C. depicting an Assyrian war chariot. The Assyrians improved the design of the chariot— putting bronze spokes in the wheels, for instance, made the chariot much faster.*

◀ *This gold ornament on a sixth to fourth century B.C. comb shows Scythian warriors in combat. The Scythians were a fierce, nomadic people from the steppes whose society was based around warfare.*

Alexander the Great (356–323 B.C.) cavalry was gradually replacing the role of the chariot.

DEFENSE AND ATTACK

Defensive walls were probably erected around the first houses and settlements ever built. The oldest fortifications yet found were built around the settlement of Jericho near the Dead Sea and date back to around 8000 B.C. Many ancient civilizations built strong defensive walls around their towns. The Mycenaean rulers, in particular, sited their towns and palaces on hills and surrounded them with thick walls constructed from huge stones.

Defensive walls prompted people to invent ways of assaulting these fortifications. The Assyrians used a

◀ *An artist's impression of the largest siege tower of ancient times, which was built in 304 B.C. by the Macedonians to besiege the Greek city-state of Rhodes. It was 130–140 ft (40–43m) high and was wheeled up to within missile range of the walls so that its large stone-thrower could destroy the defenses.*

battering ram mounted on a six-wheeled wooden frame. They also used ladders and ramps to get over walls. The ancient Greeks used a large number of siege machines, including the *sambuca*, which was a ladder that raised men to the top of the walls within the safety of a covered compartment. They also used fire-raisers, which were long wooden beams that carried cauldrons of lighted coals, sulfur, and pitch for starting fires inside the walls, and large battering rams.

Besiegers used mechanical artillery to hurl heavy missiles, such as stones and giant arrows. These devices worked either by pulling on ropes (tension) or twisting them (torsion).

ARMIES OF EMPIRE

Most empires were established and maintained through the use of military power. The three greatest armies of the ancient world were the Assyrians, the Macedonians, and the Romans.

Led by a series of warrior-kings, the Assyrians fought and defeated many of their neighbors in the Middle East and built a kingdom that stretched from the Mediterranean Sea to the Persian Gulf.

The success of the Macedonian army was largely due to their leader, Alexander the Great, who created an empire that stretched from Greece to India. The Macedonian army would only come up against a better fighting force in 197 B.C. at the battle of Cynoscephalae—a victory for the Roman legion, which supplanted the Macedonian phalanx as the ancient world's most flexible military unit.

The Roman army was the best disciplined and most organized of the ancient world. A legion was divided into cohorts and then into centuries (100 men) led by a centurion. The Romans' favored weapon was the short stabbing sword, which made them masters of hand-to-hand combat.

ALEXANDER'S ARMY

Alexander the Great was one of the greatest generals of ancient times. He began his military adventures with lightning strikes against his enemies in Greece, whom he easily conquered, then he set out to destroy the mighty Persian Empire. The core of his army was the Macedonian phalanx—a unit of foot soldiers each armed with a long pike called the *sarissa*. A heavily armed cavalry unit called the Companions was led by Alexander himself, and a lighter cavalry unit was used for scouting and speedy attacks.

Alexander inspired his men through personal courage and his ability as a leader. He had a gift for improvising under pressure and sensing when to time his attacks. He won his first major victory against the Persian army at Granicus in 334 B.C., for instance, by attacking the opposing army immediately, despite their strong position on the opposite bank of the Granicus River and the lateness of the day, and going against all advice to wait until dawn. In addition to his fighting men Alexander took with him a large number of technicians and engineers who contributed to his outstanding successes in siege warfare.

▲ *A 19th-century illustration of cavalry being overwhelmed by a Macedonian phalanx.*

SEE ALSO:

◆ **HITTITES**
◆ **ROME**
◆ **SCIENCE**
◆ **SHIPS**
◆ **STEPPE NOMADS**

WEIGHTS AND MEASURES

◀ *This wall painting from an Egyptian tomb shows metalworkers using scales to weigh gold rings. Standard weights of precious metals were used as a measure of value in much of the ancient world.*

In the ancient past people used the parts of their bodies—their fingers, hands, arms, and feet—to represent short units of measurement. They were to be the building blocks of the more complex systems of measurement that developed in later civilizations. As societies developed, reliable systems of weights and measures became important for trade, paying taxes, building, and measuring land.

As trading contacts increased, it became obvious that standardized, widely accepted systems of weighing merchandise were vital for good trading relationships. At first, small-scale transactions were based on a rough and ready "rule of thumb," but cheating was rife. Cheating was even addressed by the prophet Ezekiel in the Bible, when he said: "Enough, princes of Israel! . . . Your scales shall be honest, your bushel and your gallon shall be honest. There shall be one standard for each."

Uncovering the measurement systems used in the ancient world can be difficult. Some societies, such as ancient Egypt, left carefully inscribed measurement rods. But more often, measurements have to be figured out from the dimensions of buildings and bricks that were obviously constructed using an accepted system.

The measurement system of ancient Egypt was based on the royal cubit (forearm), a length of approximately 20.6 in. (52.3cm). Subdivisions were the palm—about 3 in. (7.5cm)—and the digit—about 0.7 in. (1.9cm). Evidence for the use of this measuring system was found on Philae Island. Here the heights of the annual floods of the Nile River were recorded on a "Nilometer"; from these measurements the scribes registered the minimum, maximum, and average levels of the Nile in cubits. Because the Nile floods washed away property boundary markers each year, surveyors were kept busy resurveying the land using ropes, which were knotted to indicate subdivisions of linear measurements.

MEASURING CORN

The official unit of corn, the *hekat*, was about 5.2 quarts (4.9l). Twenty *hekats* were equivalent to one *khar* (sack) of approximately 103.4 quarts (97.8l). The average wage of a fieldworker was one and a half *khars* per month of emmer

wheat, possibly supplemented by a small allowance of barley.

From about 1550 B.C. metals were weighed in units known as *debens*— each approximately 3.2 oz. (91g). Because there were no coins, *debens* were used as a standard of value, as this account from the New Kingdom shows:

Sold to Hay by Nebsman the Brigadier:
　1 ox, worth 120 *debens* of copper.
Received in exchange:
　2 pots of fat, value 60 *debens*;
　5 loincloths in fine cloth, worth
　　25 *debens*;
　1 vestment of southern flax, worth
　　20 *debens*;
　1 hide, worth 15 *debens*.

The value of the *deben* depended on whether the metal was copper, silver, or gold.

REEDS AND POLES

In Mesopotamia linear measurements were also based on the cubit, which was about 19.5 in. (49.5cm). The cubit

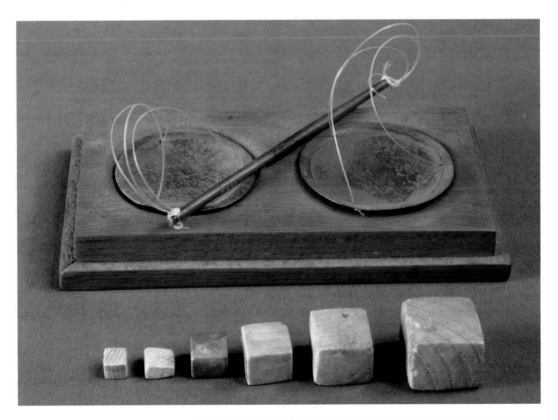

▶ *A set of weighing scales from the Indus Valley civilization. Cube-shaped stone weights such as those shown in front of the scales would have been used to weigh amounts of foodstuffs and precious metals.*

CHINESE MEASUREMENTS

Like many other ancient civilizations, the Chinese used parts of the body as units of measurement, but in no particular order and with many variations in different regions. In addition, a unit with the same name might be a different length depending on whether it was being used by a carpenter, a builder, or a tailor.

This problem was solved when Ch'in Shihuangdi, who became the first emperor of China in 221 B.C., introduced a standard system of weights and measures. The basic weight was called the *shih* or *tan* and weighed about 132 lb. (60kg). The two basic measurements of length were the *chih*, which was 9.8 in. (25cm), and the *chang*— 9.8 ft (3m). The Chinese also had a measurement for the sound made when a measuring vessel was struck. If a vessel was a uniform shape and weight, it would give a standard pitch. Measurements based on the length of a pitch pipe and its subdivisions proved more accurate than measurements based on the human body.

was subdivided into 30 digits, each of which measured about 0.6 in. (1.6cm). When they were surveying the land in order to build a ziggurat or dig a canal, Mesopotamians used larger units: the reed (6 cubits) and the pole (12 cubits). Evidence of Mesopotamian surveying skills survives on a limestone stele of Ur-Nammu, king of Ur, which shows a land-measuring cord (similar to the one used by the Egyptians) and a pair of compasses.

from finds of cube-shaped weights made of a stone called chert. The standard unit of weight was about half an ounce (14g). Historians believe that the smaller weights may have followed a binary system: 1, 2, 4, 8, 16, 32, 64. These smaller weights would have been used for weighing foodstuffs, spices, and precious metals, perhaps in a jeweler's workshop. At the other end of the scale weights probably increased as follows: 160, 200, 320,

▼ *Two Roman amphorae, pottery jars that were used to transport wine. The amphora soon became a standard measure of volume, equal to 27.7 modern quarts (26.2l).*

TALENTS AND SHEKELS

The Babylonians were the first ancient civilization to attempt to evolve a standardized system of weights and measures. From about 2400 B.C. they introduced a series of standard weights made of stone in the form of a sleeping duck. The Babylonian system of weights reflected their sexagesimal (based on the number 60) counting system. Sixty *shekels*, weighing about 0.3 oz. (8g) each, were equivalent to one *mina*, which weighed 17 oz. (480g); 60 *mina* were equivalent to one *talent*, which weighed 63.5 lb. (28.8kg). The Hittites, Assyrians, and Phoenicians all developed their measurement systems from those of the Egyptians and Babylonians.

The Indus Valley system of weights and measures has been figured out

640, 1,600, 3,200, 6,400, 8,000, 12,800.
The larger weights would have been
lifted by a rope or metal ring.

Several scales of measurement have
been found at Indus Valley excavations;
one decimal scale of 1.3 in. (3.3cm)
rises to 13.2 in. (33.5cm), which was
equivalent to the "foot" that was
widespread in western Asia. Another
find is a bronze rod marked in lengths
of 0.4 in. (0.93cm), which was probably
the equivalent of a half-digit. Sixty half-
digits make up a cubit of about 22 in.
(55.8cm). It is possible to see, by
measuring excavated Indus buildings,
that these units of measurement were
actually used in construction. There is
a consistency in weights and measures,
and even in brick sizes, at sites
throughout the Indus region. This
indicates that a central authority
probably imposed a system across a
wide area of the Indus Valley.

ROMAN MEASUREMENTS

The Romans, like the Greeks before
them, based their measurements of
length on, in ascending order, the
finger's breadth (*digitus*), the palm, and
the foot (*pes*), which was equivalent to
about 11.6 in. (29.57cm). Longer units
of measurement reflect the importance
of Rome's marching army: 5 *pedes*
equal one *passus* (pace), while 1,000
passus are equivalent to one Roman
mile—0.9 miles (1.5km).

Accurate measurements and land
surveys were vital tools in Rome's
imperial expansion. Land surveyors
used two main instruments, the *groma*
(cross-staff) and the *decempeda* (10-
foot rod). Using these instruments,
newly acquired imperial territory was
measured, mapped, and allocated,
usually to ex-soldiers or privileged
civilians. Military surveyors were
responsible for planning fortifications
and roads, and they worked with a
great degree of accuracy.

▲ *This sculpture
from the second
century B.C.
shows a Roman
tradesman using
a set of scales to
weigh goods.
Uniform systems
of weights and
measures were
developed in the
ancient world
largely to make
trading easier.*

The long-distance trade networks of
the Roman world are reflected in the
measurements they used for capacity.
For measurement of liquid the smallest
unit was the *cochlearia* ("spoonful"),
while the amphora was equivalent to
approximately 27.7 quarts (26.2l).
Amphorae were pottery vessels that
were used to transport wine and oil all
over the empire, mainly by sea. The
largest measurement of dry goods was
the *modius*—approximately 104.4
quarts (98.7l)—the name given to
the cylindrical containers used for
transporting corn.

SEE ALSO:

◆ **MOHENJODARO**
◆ **MONEY AND WEALTH**
◆ **NUMBERS AND COUNTING**
◆ **TITHES AND TAXES**
◆ **TRADE**

WOMEN

ΚΑΛΛΙΡΟΟΣ ΝΗΙΔΕΣΙ ΚΡΗΝΗ ΗΔ ΑΦΙΕΡΟΥΤΑΙ·

From earliest times it appears that men and women had different roles. In hunter-gatherer communities men were the hunters and might be away from base for short or long periods. The women left behind gathered wild foods such as nuts, roots, and fruits. They also looked after the children, prepared and preserved food, and made clothes from the hides of slaughtered animals.

Women were the core of prehistoric society, and scholars believe that for many thousands of years societies were predominantly matriarchal. This meant that the mother was head of the family and that inheritance went through the female line. Most of the earliest sculptural images in Europe and Anatolia (modern-day Turkey) represent a mother goddess, indicating that women were honored for their birth-giving role. As people began to settle and farm around 8000 B.C., the cult of the mother goddess continued in many early farming villages.

REDUCED POWERS

Reverence for women persisted in a much reduced form in the early urban societies of Mesopotamia and Egypt. In Babylonia the law code of King Hammurabi (around 1760 B.C.) set out

▲ *A 19th-century picture showing Greek women drawing water from a well and taking the opportunity to chat with friends. Poorer women had to do their own housework, which also gave them more freedom than wealthy women, who had to stay in their homes.*

SPECIALIZED SKILLS

Women's knowledge of plants meant that they were often responsible for medicinal herbal potions. At the site of Monte Verde in southern Chile, which was occupied 12,500 years ago, a range of 22 medicinal plants have been found in a separate hut, almost certainly the home of a medicine woman. Frequently a woman could use her skills at certain crafts to bring her a more powerful position within the society. Among the Native Americans of the Plains a woman's skill at tanning, stretching, and softening animal hides and fashioning them into clothes and shoes brought both status and wealth to her family.

a number of laws concerning the status of women. Women were subjected to arranged marriages, and the groom had to pay the bride's father a bride-price. However, the bride-price and the bride's dowry then became the wife's property, which she was entitled to pass on to her children.

The cult of the goddess was important in many early farming villages

If a wife had no children, she had the right to select a suitable woman to bear children for her husband. If her husband wanted to divorce her, she automatically kept custody of any children, and he had to pay for their upbringing. All these measures ensured that women retained a measure of independence. Women who did not marry could devote their life to religion, becoming high priestesses and temple maidens at the shrines of deities such as the Babylonian goddess Ishtar.

EGYPTIAN WOMEN

In Egypt, although women were able to become pharaohs and priests, they were not allowed to become officials, and very few of them became scribes. However, most other occupations,

▶ *A Neolithic clay statue of a mother and child, found in Serbia. In early times women were greatly respected for their role as mothers.*

WOMAN WARRIOR

The rich and well-preserved burial of Fu Hao, royal consort to the 13th-century B.C. Shang king Wu Ding, has revealed a great deal about the life of women in the Shang court. Fu Hao was held in particularly high esteem by both the king and the state, and became one of the greatest military leaders in Shang China. She led campaigns against neighboring tribes, commanding an army of over 13,000 soldiers. She also performed ritual ceremonies in which the spirits of ancestors were consulted on all affairs of state, a mark of the king's great trust in her. Her grave contained over 1,600 objects, including weapons, many bronze vessels used in rituals and ceremonies, and personal items, such as 527 hairpins—a sign that elaborate hairstyles must have been common among high-status women.

▼ *This stone relief from Susa in Persia (modern-day Iran) dates from the eighth century B.C. and shows a woman spinning.*

including running businesses, were open to them. At all levels of Egyptian society wives were entitled to own land and property, and marriage contracts frequently gave the husband's property in its entirety to his wife. Women could also purchase land and own slaves.

China's first urban civilization, the Shang, developed around the valley of the Yellow River from about 1500 B.C. Inscriptions on Shang oracle bones used in divination refer to King Wu Ding, one of the greatest rulers of the Shang dynasty, and his many wives.

Traditionally, in China it was believed that a woman's main responsibility was to rear children and take care of the home. Military action and participation in religious rituals was considered to be the preserve of the men. But over 20 of Wu Ding's consorts were directly involved in the organization of farming, fishing, and animal breeding, as well as in rituals and military activities.

INDIAN WOMEN

Nothing is known of the status of women in the early urban civilizations of the Indus Valley, although later Indian society was matriarchal. However, around 1000–500 B.C. Vedic invaders from the north introduced a more male-dominated society where women were subject to their fathers and husbands. Nevertheless, women still had some control over their own property and could own businesses. Although they could not become priests, they could become nuns.

In some parts of India a high-born widow was expected to commit suttee—that is, throw herself on the funeral pyre of her dead husband so that she too died in order to be a companion to him in his afterlife.

GREEK WOMEN

In the city-states that flourished in Greece from the eighth century B.C. onward there was increasing emphasis on civic life—men lived their lives in public, spending most of their time in the *agora* (town square), the council chamber, gymnasium, library, theater, or temples. Athenian women, on the other hand, were called citizens but had no independent status. They could not own property and were under the protection of a *kyrios* (guardian), usually their father or husband. A woman's marriage dowry came under the complete control of her husband. A woman could not even inherit

▲ *A group of female musicians playing at the Chinese court, shown on a silk scroll painting from the 10th century A.D.*

property; if her husband died, she was forced, by law, to marry her closest male relative.

Wealthy Athenian women spent most of their lives in the segregated female quarters of their homes. Vase paintings of the sixth to fourth centuries B.C. give a vivid picture of women's life; they are shown bathing, grooming themselves, nursing children, spinning, and weaving. They seldom left their homes except to take part in religious festivities or to visit relatives' graves. Less wealthy women were subjected to fewer restrictions; they worked with their husbands or were employed as servants in wealthy households.

THE WOMEN OF GHANA

The kingdom of Ghana flourished between the Niger and Senegal rivers in the eighth century A.D. The women of its capital Kumbi Saleh and of other trading cities of the region were treated with great respect; some held government posts and were even allowed to wear collars and bracelets, which were usually worn only by the king. Women at all levels of society were permitted to be naked in public, which was a sign of freedom rather than having any sexual implications. In the town of Walata wives were allowed to take lovers and the throne was inherited by the son of the king's sister rather than by the son of the king.

SPARTAN FREEDOMS

The life of women in Sparta was very different from that of the other Greek city-states. Family life was not considered important, and boys left home to live permanently in military schools from the age of seven. Girls stayed at home with their mothers but were encouraged to live vigorous outdoor lives, participating in sports such as running, wrestling, and javelin-throwing, and wearing short tunics that shocked other Greeks. When they married, they ran the home, and their husbands continued to live in military barracks. By the third century B.C. about two-thirds of Spartan land was owned by women, putting them in an extremely powerful position.

▼ *Egyptian women dressed up for a feast, with perfumed cones of fat on their heads.*

Although women were oppressed in Republican Rome (509–27 B.C.), by the time of the Imperial era reforms had given them some protection. They retained their legal identity when they married and were able to own, inherit, and dispose of their own property. But their social role was to stay at home and bear and bring up children. If they were wealthy, their slaves did most of the domestic duties. Lower-class women shared their husband's work, specializing in fine crafts such as silver-working and perfumery. The spread of literacy benefited some wealthy women. If they could get an education, they could become doctors or teachers or exercise a powerful political influence on their husbands.

VIKING WOMEN

The daily life of Viking women was typical of the lives of many women in north Europe in the first millennium A.D. They milked cows, churned butter, dried fish, spun and dyed wool, wove cloth, and looked after their children. When their husbands left on trading or

▶ *This first-century B.C. fresco (wall painting) from the Roman city of Pompeii shows a woman artist painting a portrait. Wealthy Roman women enjoyed a large amount of freedom. While slaves carried out domestic duties, their mistresses were free to attend public functions, visit friends, and develop their artistic abilities.*

raiding expeditions, they had full responsibility for running the home. Sometimes, they uprooted themselves and their families and followed their husbands to war, where they were responsible for feeding the soldiers and tending to their wounds. Viking women were allowed some say in choosing a husband and were also allowed to retain both their dowry and bride price after they were married. They were permitted to divorce their husbands, and their marriage contracts indicated that in the case of a divorce, the property was divided equally between husband and wife.

A VOICE FROM THE PAST

This was the epitaph on a Roman tombstone for a woman called Veturia:

❝ My father was Veturius. My husband was Fortunatus. I lived 27 years, and I was married for 16 years to the same man. After giving birth to six children, only one of whom lived, I died. ❞

SEE ALSO:

◆ CHILDREN
◆ DAILY LIFE
◆ INDIA
◆ MARRIAGE AND FAMILIES

WRITING

The invention of writing was one of the most important steps in human progress. It was a powerful tool of government, used for recording laws and rulers' decrees. Writing was a means of communicating easily and reliably over long distances and became a vital part of international trade, diplomacy, and administration. It could also be used to record historical events, set down myths and other oral traditions, and create new literary works.

Without writing it was difficult for a civilization to store its past learning and to pass it on to future generations. At first only a small group of people—scribes, officials, and priests—were able to read and write, but by the time of the ancient Greeks and Romans many ordinary people were able to understand and use the written word.

The world's first writing system was developed by the Sumerians of Mesopotamia. Farmers working the rich soil of the Euphrates and Tigris river valleys began to produce surplus produce, which was stored in temple

▲ *This Egyptian painting dating from 2494–2345 B.C. shows two scribes with their papyrus rolls and reed pens. At first reed pens were chewed at the end to form a brush-like tip, but by the third century B.C. the tip was pointed.*

THE ROSETTA STONE

In 1798 Napoleon Bonaparte of France invaded Egypt. While building fortifications at Rosetta in 1799, some of his soldiers uncovered a black basalt stone that was to transform studies of ancient Egyptian civilization. It was inscribed with the same text in two languages (ancient Egyptian and Greek) and in three scripts—hieroglyphic, demotic (or everyday) Egyptian, and Greek—and it celebrated the first anniversary of the coronation of Ptolemy V in 196 B.C. The Greek script was to provide the key to understanding the Egyptian. The French scholar Jean François Champollion (1790–1832) was the first person to realize the significance of phonetic (sound) symbols in interpreting the hieroglyphics. He was able to translate the hieroglyphic section of the Rosetta Stone in its entirety; and when sent a copy of the carved inscriptions at the Egyptian temple of Abu Simbel, he found he was able to understand them. He began to write the first Egyptian grammar (completed after his death by his brother), a work that unlocked a treasure trove of Egyptian texts, which could at last be read after thousands of years of darkness. The Rosetta Stone has been on display in the British Museum, London, since 1802.

warehouses. Soon it became essential to keep an accurate record of supplies. Also, as long-distance trading networks extended across the Middle East, it became important to be able to keep records of trading transactions. From about 8000 B.C. clay counting tokens were used to represent goods. By the fourth millennium B.C. the tokens were being sealed into clay envelopes that were marked with signs indicating their contents—the first written symbols.

FIRST WRITING SYSTEM

These abstract signs evolved into the world's first writing system around 3300 B.C. Initially, Sumerian script was pictographic; pictures represented words. This system proved both limited and cumbersome, and so symbols gradually came to represent ideas (ideograms). For example, a pictograph of a mouth could also be used as a symbol representing the verb "to speak."

The next stage was to develop symbols that indicated the sounds of the spoken language. To begin with, the Sumerians took advantage of the fact that many words sound the same, although they have a quite different meaning. Just as in English the word "belief" could be represented by pictures of a bee and a leaf, so in Sumerian the words for life and arrow sounded the same, and "life" was represented by a pictogram of an arrow. Later, the system included symbols that indicated the sounds of the language (consonants and vowels).

Scribes wrote with a hollow-reed stylus on wet clay tablets. The marks were wedge-shaped; and because the

▼ *One of the 20,000 clay tablets in cuneiform script found in the archives of the royal palace of Ebla (in Syria), which was built about 2500 B.C.*

Latin for wedge is *cuneus*, Sumerian writing was called cuneiform. At the end of the second millennium B.C. the Sumerian civilization gave way to that of the Assyrians and the Babylonians, who adopted and elaborated the cuneiform system of writing. Later it spread throughout the Middle East to the eastern Mediterranean coast and as far west as Persia.

EGYPTIAN WRITING

The Greeks called Egyptian writing hieroglyphs (meaning sacred carvings) because it was used for inscriptions on temples, tombs, and monuments. The Egyptian writing system, which appeared from about 3100 B.C. onward, was unique, although it was influenced by Sumerian writing. Like the Sumerian system, it involved a combination of pictograms (where symbols represent words) and hieroglyphs, which represented consonants or groups of consonants. Hieroglyphs were not Egypt's only script; they evolved into two flowing scripts called Egyptian hieratic and demotic that could be written much more quickly than hieroglyphs, using ink and a reed pen. Writing was used to administer and record every aspect of daily life, from farming produce to land surveys, court cases, and royal decrees.

PAPYRUS RECORDS

Much ancient Egyptian writing is preserved on papyrus, which was made from the flattened inner layers of the stems of papyrus plants that grew along the shores of the Nile River.

The earliest surviving papyrus is over 5,000 years old. Highly trained professional scribes studied the art of writing for 10 to 12 years, practicing on slabs of limestone (because papyrus was too precious to waste). Their reward for this long education was a highly privileged position in Egyptian society

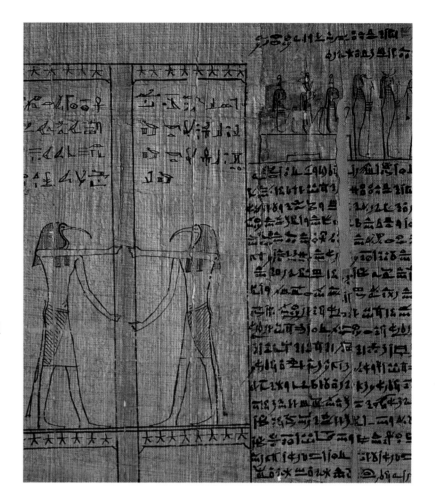

and exemption from paying taxes. The ability to write was essential for careers in the higher ranks of the army, the palace, medicine, or the priesthood.

CHINESE WRITING

No one knows when writing began in ancient China; the earliest examples to survive date from the Shang dynasty (1766–1100 B.C.). The writing was found on oracle bones, fragments of animal bones that were heated to produce cracks. These cracks were interpreted by a diviner in much the same way that people read tea leaves today. The predictions were then inscribed onto the oracle bones.

The Chinese writing system was a complex combination of pictograms, ideograms, and signs that indicated sounds. There are more than 50,000 Chinese signs, or characters. They have changed very little over the last 4,000

▲ *A section from an* Egyptian **Book of the Dead** *written on papyrus. The text above the illustrations is in hieroglyphs, and the text on the right is written in hieratic script.*

▶ *This ninth-century* A.D. *Viking stone is engraved with lines of runes, a form of writing used by early Germanic peoples.*

WRITING MATERIALS

The earliest materials used to write on were clay (Middle East), bone and shell (China), palm leaves and birch bark (India), and cotton (Egypt). By approximately 3000 B.C. the Egyptians had begun writing on sheets or rolls of papyrus. It became the most widely used writing material of ancient times. When the pharaohs banned the sale of papyrus to other countries in the second century B.C., the shortage of writing materials led to the invention of parchment in the city of Pergamum (in modern Turkey). Parchment was made from the prepared skins of animals, and it gradually became more popular than papyrus. The Chinese had been using silk, bamboo strips, and wooden tablets to write on, but in about 200 A.D. they invented paper. The Maya also invented paper, made from fig bark, in the fifth century, but the art of papermaking did not spread to Europe until about the eighth century A.D.

Plant juices and mineral pigments have been used as paints or inks since prehistoric times by many societies. Writing inks date from about 2500 B.C. in both Egypt and China. A mixture of lampblack (soot collected from burning lamps) and liquid gum or glue was molded into sticks and allowed to dry. Before use, the sticks were moistened with water on an ink stone. The Sumerians and Egyptians used sharpened reeds as pens. The Chinese were writing with brushes by the first millennium B.C. The Maya also used brushes or feather pens. Feather pens were the forerunners of the quill pens that would revolutionize writing in the sixth century A.D.

years, making ancient Chinese texts quite easy to interpret, in contrast to many other ancient writing systems. The Chinese writing system spread over much of East Asia.

ALPHABETS

The alphabetic system is the most common form of writing in the world today. Alphabets use a limited number of letters to represent consonants and vowels, which can then be combined together to form words. This compact system involves learning only 26 letters to write all the words in the English language—a much easier system than the 800 cuneiform signs or several thousand Chinese characters.

It is probable that the earliest forms of alphabetic systems were evolving on the coast of the eastern Mediterranean around 1400 B.C. The Phoenicians, a maritime trading people whose base was the coast of modern Syria and Lebanon, had evolved an alphabetic system by 1100 B.C. that used only 22 characters, each representing a consonant. But it was the Greeks who, in the eighth century B.C., developed the world's first truly alphabetic system, with letters representing both vowels and consonants. Phoenicians and Greeks had close trading contacts, especially in the eastern Mediterranean, where the Greeks encountered the Phoenician writing system. They took on the Phoenician alphabet, which had too many consonant symbols for their own language, and used the extra symbols to stand for vowel sounds.

The Etruscans, who lived in western central Italy in the seventh century B.C., adapted the Greek alphabetic script and introduced their alphabet to the region of Latium and its Latin-speaking inhabitants. Several changes had to be made to accommodate the Latin language including, in the first

◄ *This section of a carved wood doorway comes from a Mayan temple at Tikal (in modern Guatemala). It shows a Mayan lord and a panel of glyphs (the Mayan form of writing). Mayan writing is read in double columns from left to right and from top to bottom.*

THE GREEK ALPHABET

An alphabet is a system of writing that expresses the sounds of a language with a few simple signs. The first civilization to evolve an alphabet with both consonants and vowels was ancient Greece. The Greeks adapted the earlier 22 letter alphabet of the Phoenicians, which only had consonants. Our alphabet is a modernized version of the Latin alphabet, which was adapted from the Greek. Cyrillic, which is used in Russia and parts of Eastern Europe, also evolved from the Greek alphabet with some extra letters added.

α	β	γ	δ	ε	ζ	η	θ
alpha	beta	gamma	delta	epsilon	zeta	eta	theta
a	**b**	**g**	**d**	**e**	**z**	**e**	**th**
ι	κ	λ	μ	ν	ξ	ο	π
iota	kappa	lambda	mu	nu	xi	omicron	pi
i	**k**	**l**	**m**	**n**	**x/ks**	**o**	**p**
ρ	σ	τ	υ	φ	χ	ψ	ω
rho	sigma	tau	upsilon	phi	chi	psi	omega
r	**s**	**t**	**u**	**f/ph**	**ch**	**ps**	**o**

▲ *This table shows each letter of the Greek alphabet with the name of the letter underneath it, and then its English sound.*

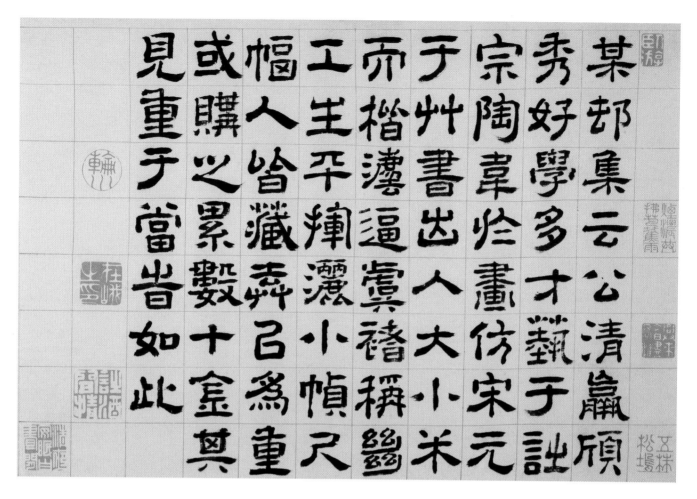

century B.C., the introduction of the letters Y and Z. As the Romans colonized the Italian peninsula and then built their empire, the influence of the Latin alphabet extended well beyond the borders of Italy.

ALTERNATIVE ALPHABETS

By the second century A.D. in Britain and Ireland the Celts had developed an alphabetic script called Ogham that consisted of 20 linear characters, while the Germanic peoples were using a runic system consisting of 24 symbols arranged in an alphabetic order called a futhark after the first six characters (f, u, th, a, r, k). But as the Romans advanced farther into northern Europe, these scripts were forced to give way to Latin. The arrival and spread of Christianity reinforced the importance of Latin, and it became the written language of the monasteries.

The Maya, who flourished in Central America around 300–900 A.D., developed their own unique system of writing, which is still being deciphered by scholars today. Mayan symbols, or glyphs, combined pictograms with syllabic symbols. Inscriptions carved in stone recorded key facts about royalty and wars. Four books called codices, written on tree bark paper, have also survived. Other Mesoamerican peoples, such as the Aztecs and Mixtecs, also developed their own scripts.

SEE ALSO:

◆ EDUCATION
◆ LANGUAGE
◆ LEARNING
◆ LITERATURE
◆ MINOANS

▲ *Chinese script was the basis of all Eastern writing systems, and until the 18th century more than half of all the world's books had been written in Chinese. This 17th-century Chinese text is written in ink on paper.*

TIMELINE

	6500 BC	6000	5500	5000	4500	4000	3500

EUROPE

NEOLITHIC EUROPE: MEGALITHIC MONUMENTS 6500—1500 B
STEPPES: SREDNY STOG 4400—3500

OCEANIA

◄ ABORIGINE CULTURE 40,000 B.C.—PRESENT

**INDIA AND
THE FAR EAST**

AMERICAS

◄ JERICHO 10,000—6000 B.C.
ÇATAL HÖYÜK 6250—5400 B.C.

MESOPOTAMIA 5000—3000 B.C.

**MIDDLE EAST
AND AFRICA**

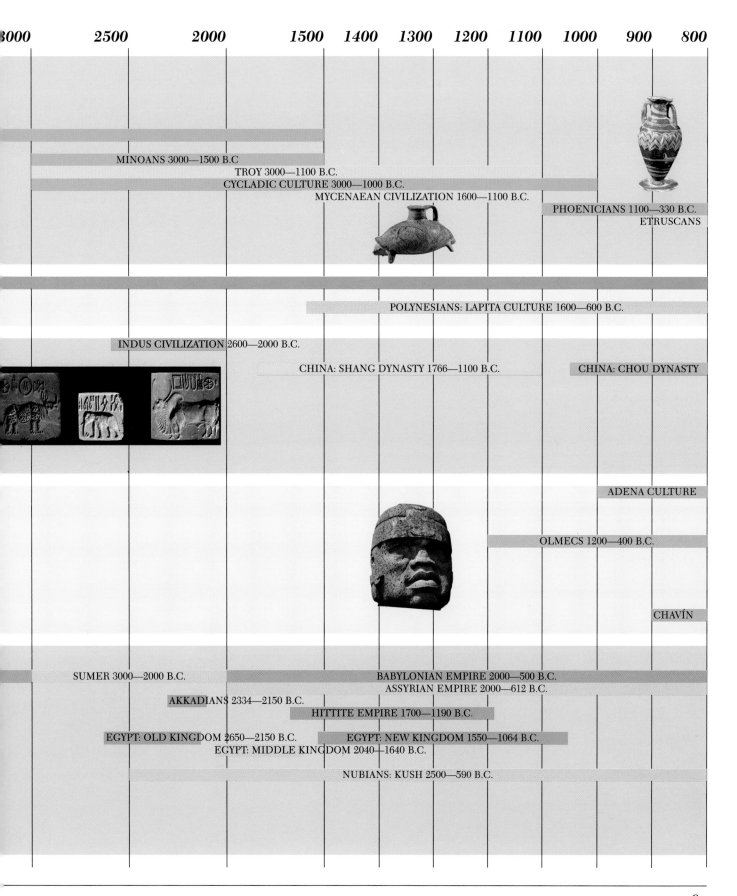

3000 2500 2000 1500 1400 1300 1200 1100 1000 900 800

MINOANS 3000—1500 B.C

TROY 3000—1100 B.C.

CYCLADIC CULTURE 3000—1000 B.C.

MYCENAEAN CIVILIZATION 1600—1100 B.C.

PHOENICIANS 1100—330 B.C.

ETRUSCANS

POLYNESIANS: LAPITA CULTURE 1600—600 B.C.

INDUS CIVILIZATION 2600—2000 B.C.

CHINA: SHANG DYNASTY 1766—1100 B.C.

CHINA: CHOU DYNASTY

ADENA CULTURE

OLMECS 1200—400 B.C.

CHAVÍN

SUMER 3000—2000 B.C.

BABYLONIAN EMPIRE 2000—500 B.C.

ASSYRIAN EMPIRE 2000—612 B.C.

AKKADIANS 2334—2150 B.C.

HITTITE EMPIRE 1700—1190 B.C.

EGYPT: OLD KINGDOM 2650—2150 B.C.

EGYPT: NEW KINGDOM 1550—1064 B.C.

EGYPT: MIDDLE KINGDOM 2040—1640 B.C.

NUBIANS: KUSH 2500—590 B.C.

800 BC   700   600   500   400   300   200   100   AD 1   100   200   300   40

CELTIC CULTURE 500 B.C.—50 A.D.

PHOENICIANS 1100—330 B.C.

ETRUSCANS 900—250 B.C.

GREECE 800—338 B.C.

ROMAN REPUBLIC 509—27 B.C.

ROMAN EMPIRE 27 B.C.—476 A.D.

ABORIGINE CULTURE 40,000 B.C.—PRESENT DAY

POLYNESIANS: LAPITA CULTURE

POLYNESIAN COLONIZATION OF PACIFIC 300 B.C.—1000 A.D.

INDIA: MAURYAN EMPIRE 320—185 B.C.

INDIA: GUP

CHINA: CHOU DYNASTY 1050—256 B.C.

CHINA: HAN DYNASTY 202 B.C.—220 A.D.

SOUTHEAST ASIA: DONG SON CULTURE 500 B.C.—43 A.D.

KOREA

ADENA CULTURE 1000 B.C.—100 A.D.

SOUTHWESTERN PEOPLES 250 B.C.—1450

HOPEWELL CULTURE 100 B.C.—500 A.D.

OLMECS 1200—400 B.C.

TEOTIHUACÁN 200 B.C.—650 A.D.

CHAVÍN CULTURE 900—200 B.C.

MOCHE CULTURE 50 B.C.—750 A.D.

PERSIAN EMPIRE 550—331 B.C.

BABYLONIAN EMPIRE 2000—500 B.C.

ASSYRIAN EMPIRE 2000—612 B.C.

NUBIANS: KUSH 2500—590 B.C.

NUBIANS: MEROE 590 B.C.—350 A.D.

NU

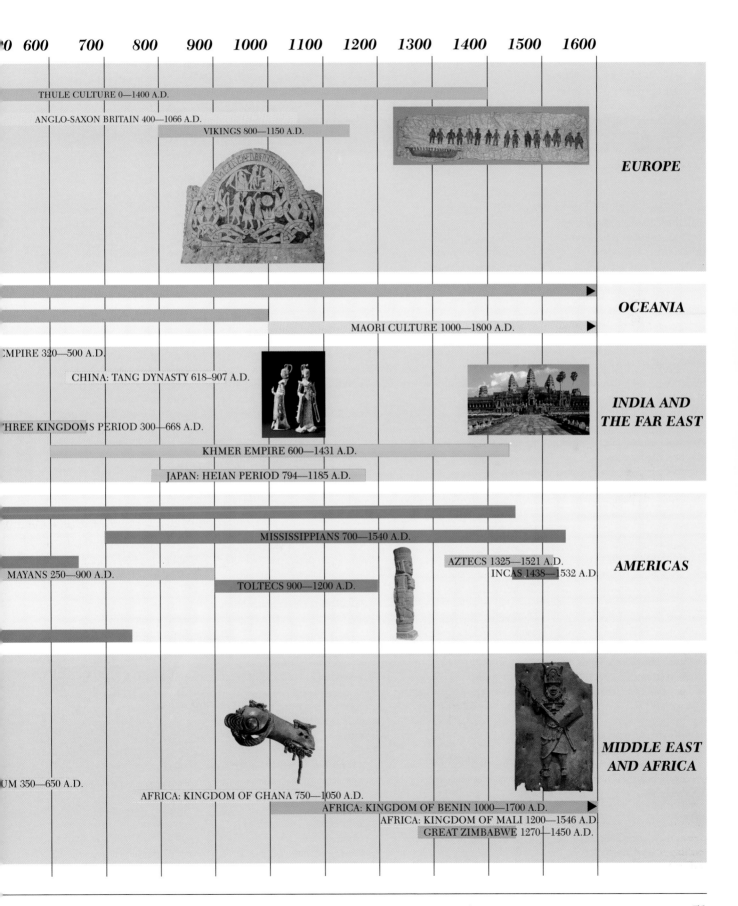

600 700 800 900 1000 1100 1200 1300 1400 1500 1600

THULE CULTURE 0—1400 A.D.

ANGLO-SAXON BRITAIN 400—1066 A.D.

VIKINGS 800—1150 A.D.

EUROPE

OCEANIA

MAORI CULTURE 1000—1800 A.D.

EMPIRE 320—500 A.D.

CHINA: TANG DYNASTY 618–907 A.D.

THREE KINGDOMS PERIOD 300—668 A.D.

INDIA AND THE FAR EAST

KHMER EMPIRE 600—1431 A.D.

JAPAN: HEIAN PERIOD 794—1185 A.D.

MISSISSIPPIANS 700—1540 A.D.

AZTECS 1325—1521 A.D.

INCAS 1438—1532 A.D.

MAYANS 250—900 A.D.

AMERICAS

TOLTECS 900—1200 A.D.

MIDDLE EAST AND AFRICA

UM 350—650 A.D.

AFRICA: KINGDOM OF GHANA 750—1050 A.D.

AFRICA: KINGDOM OF BENIN 1000—1700 A.D.

AFRICA: KINGDOM OF MALI 1200—1546 A.D.

GREAT ZIMBABWE 1270—1450 A.D.

GLOSSARY

A.D. Anno Domini ("the year of our Lord") was the year that Christ was born. All dates with these letters written after them are measured forward from his birth to the present day.

awl A pointed tool for making small holes in leather, wood, and other items.

B.C. Before Christ. All dates with these letters written after them are measured backward from Christ's birth date.

Bronze Age The period of human history when bronze tools were first used. In Europe and Asia it lasted from around 2000 to 700 B.C.

bureaucracy A governing body organized into a number of separate departments, each specializing in a different area.

ceramic An object made from clay or a similar material, usually by firing it in an oven.

city-state An independent city that rules territories that are subject to it.

consolidate To unite parts into a whole, or to strengthen one's power over a state.

consort A husband or wife, particularly of a ruler.

culture The beliefs, kinds of family relationships, art forms, and patterns of behavior shared by a society.

cuneiform An ancient system of writing made up of wedge-shaped characters, especially that used in Mesopotamia.

decipher To discover the meaning of something (such as writing or a language) that is difficult to read or understand.

diadem A crown, usually made from precious materials.

domesticate Taking animals and plants out of the wild and changing them so that they become adaptable to human needs, to be used for food, materials, or transportation.

dynasty A series of rulers from the same family.

economy The resources and finances of a community or country, especially when they are managed by a central government.

embalm To treat a dead body with substances that will preserve it.

epitaph An inscription on a tomb or gravestone about the person buried there.

freeman A person who is neither a slave nor a servant but is free.

fresco A wall painting made with water-based paints on fresh plaster.

funerary Items or places, such as tombs, associated with the burial of a dead person.

hierarchy The division of a social group into ranks or classes.

hunter-gatherers People in the Stone Age who existed by hunting wild animals and gathering berries, roots, nuts, and fruit.

inscribe To mark a surface with words or characters.

Iron Age The third period of mankind, after the Bronze Age, when iron was the main metal used. In Europe it lasted from about 700 B.C. to 100 A.D.

irrigation A man-made system for bringing water to the land to help plants grow that was first developed in about 4500 B.C. in Mesopotamia.

linear measure Any unit or system for measuring length.

lyre A stringed musical instrument played by ancient peoples, consisting of a sound-box and two curved arms connected at the top.

Mesoamerican Describes the ancient civilizations that flourished in Central America in the region stretching from central Mexico to present-day Nicaragua.

metallurgy The method of either working with, or heating, metals in order to make new types and shapes.

millennium A period of 1,000 years.

molten To turn metal liquid by heating.

Neolithic Of the later Stone Age, when people started to farm and live in settlements.

Paleolithic Of the early Stone Age, when people first began to use stone tools. The Paleolithic period began around 2.5 million years ago and ended around 10,000 B.C.

papyrus A writing material made from an aquatic Egyptian plant.

parchment A writing material made from prepared animal skins.

philosopher A person who constructs theories on the meaning of human life and other profound issues.

relief A sculpture that is carved into the side of a wall so that it projects out of a flat background surface.

sack To plunder, or rob, and partly destroy a place.

sarcophagus A coffin, usually stone, often decorated with writing or sculpture.

scavenge To search for or find something usable from discarded material.

scribe Before the invention of printing a person employed to copy documents by hand.

segregate To keep people apart, usually because of their race or sex.

smelting The method used to separate a metal from its ore. It involves heating the ore to a very high temperature.

staple A basic food item or crop.

Stone Age The first period of mankind, before the invention of metal, when people used stone tools and weapons. In Europe it occurred between about 2.5 million and 2000 B.C.

stupa A domed or bell-shaped Buddhist monument that usually contains sacred items.

supplement Something added to complete a thing, or to give a bit extra.

symbol Something that stands for something else. For instance, a cross often symbolizes Christianity.

tribute A payment of gifts, money, or people, usually on a regular basis, by one state or ruler to another to show submission or loyalty.

Further Reading

Andrews, Anthony P. *First Cities*. Washington, DC: Smithsonian Books, 1995.

Brewer, Paul. *Warfare in the Ancient World*. Austin, Texas: Raintree/Steck Vaughn, 1998.

Brown, Dale M. (editor). *Sumer: Cities of Eden*. Alexandria, Virginia: Time-Life Books, 1993.

Clare, John D. (editor). *The Vikings*. San Diego: Harcourt Brace Jovanovich, 1992.

Connolly, Peter, and Hazel Dodge. *The Ancient City: Life in Classical Athens and Rome*. Oxford: Oxford University Press, 1998.

Ganeri, Anita. *The Story of Weights and Measures*. Oxford: Oxford University Press, 1997.

Geography Department, Runestone Press. *Sold! The Origins of Money and Trade*. Minneapolis, Minnesota: Runestone Press, 1994.

Gonen, Rivka. *Charge! Weapons and Warfare in Ancient Times*. Minneapolis, Minnesota: Runestone Press, 1993.

Hicks, Peter. *Troy and Knossos*. Austin, Texas: Raintree Steck-Vaughn, 1997.

James, Simon. *Ancient Rome*. New York: Viking Press, 1992.

Kenoyer, Jonathan Mark. *Ancient Cities of the Indus Valley Civilization*. Oxford: Oxford University Press, 1998.

Martell, Hazel Mary, Ivan Stalio, and Francesca D'Ottavi. *Myths and Civilization of the Vikings*. New York: Peter Bedrick Books, 1998.

Martell, Hazel Mary. *Over 6,000 Years Ago: In the Stone Age*. New York: New Discovery Books, 1992.

Morley, Jacqueline, and Mark Bergin. *Viking Town*. New York: Franklin Watts, Inc., 1999.

Murdoch, David, Christopher Forsay, and Anne Yvonne Gilbert. *Tutankhamun: The Life and Death of a Pharaoh*. New York: DK Publishing, 1998.

Robinson, Andrew. *The Story of Writing*. London: Thames & Hudson, 1995.

Samoyault, Tiphaine, and Kathryn M. Pulver. *Alphabetical Order: How the Alphabet Began*. New York: Viking Children's Books, 1998.

Tyler, Deborah. *The Greeks and Troy*. New York: Dillon Press, 1993.

Whittaker, John C. *Flintknapping: Making and Understanding Stone Tools*. Austin, Texas: University of Texas Press, 1994.

Set Index

For David and Paul

American edition published in 2017 by Andersen Press USA,
an imprint of Andersen Press Ltd.
www.andersenpressusa.com

First published in Great Britain in 2017 by Andersen Press Ltd.,
20 Vauxhall Bridge Road, London SW1V 2SA.

Copyright © Ciara Flood, 2017

Distributed in the United States and Canada by
Lerner Publishing Group, Inc.
241 First Avenue North
Minneapolis, MN 55401 USA
For reading levels and more information, look up this title at www.lernerbooks.com.

Printed and bound in China.

Library of Congress Cataloging-in-Publication Data Available.
ISBN 978-1-5124-8122-8
eBook ISBN 978-1-5124-8131-0

1-TL-7/15/2017

Ciara Flood

There's a WALRUS in My Bed!

Andersen Press USA

Flynn was very excited about sleeping in his new bed.

But there was one rather large problem.

"Mom, Dad, there's a walrus in my bed," said Flynn.

"You must have been dreaming," said Dad.

"But there really, really is!"

"You know it's naughty to tell fibs," said Mom.

Flynn sighed and went back to his bedroom.

Flynn was trying to squeeze
into the bed when he heard
a very loud noise coming
from Walrus's tummy.

RuuMM

MBLE

"Are you hungry?" he asked Walrus.

"**Harrumph!**" said Walrus.

Flynn wasn't sure what walruses liked to eat.

He hoped it wasn't little children.

"Flynn, it's far too late
for snacks," said Mom.
"But they're not for me,
they're for Walrus," Flynn told her.

Walrus ate all the snacks.
He didn't seem hungry any more,
but he wasn't sleepy either.

sneezed Walrus.

"Do you have a cold?" Flynn asked.
"Harrumph!" sniffed Walrus.

Flynn got some extra blankets.

Walrus started to get hot and cranky.

"Oh dear," said Flynn.

"You must be really sick."

"Harrumph!"

wheezed Walrus.

"Walrus isn't feeling well – he needs
a glass of milk," said Flynn.
"Perhaps Walrus shouldn't have eaten
all those snacks," Dad muttered.

After drinking the milk,

Walrus had to use the bathroom.

"I know you're a little nervous about your new bed,"

said Mom, "but it's way past your bedtime."

"It's not me who won't go to sleep,"

grumbled Flynn. "It's Walrus!"

"OK, Walrus, that's enough
messing around!" said Flynn.
"I'm going to sing you to sleep."
"Harrumph!" said Walrus,
who still looked wide awake.

"Is the room too dark?"

"Harrumph!"

"Or too bright?"

"Harrumph!"

"Are you scared of monsters?"

"Harrumph!"

"Or do you have an itch you can't reach?"

Flynn had a long,
hard think.

"Maybe what you
really need is..."

"... a cuddle!"

Walrus closed his eyes,
gave a great, big

YAA

AAWWN

and finally fell asleep.

Flynn snuggled down beside him.

But there was still one rather large problem...

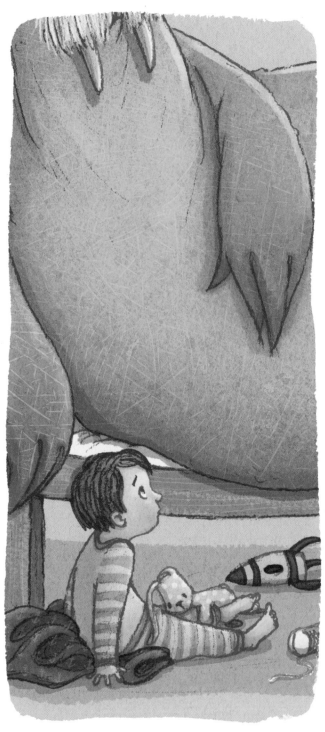

the bed just wasn't big enough for both of them.
Flynn tiptoed into Mom and Dad's bedroom.

"Mom, Dad," he whispered,
"Can Walrus sleep in your bed tonight?"
"If we say yes will you promise to go
to sleep?" asked Mom. Flynn nodded.
"Yes!!" they both shouted.

Flynn stretched out in his soft, warm bed.

"Night night, Walrus," he said.

"Harrumph!" said Walrus.

And at last, everyone could go to sleep.

Well, almost everyone.